Psychology Revivals

Letters to Margaret

First published in 1941, the original blurb for *Letters to Margaret* reads: 'In view of the almost universal ignorance of the most elementary biological and psychological facts of life amongst adults, and waste of time and energy amongst children in attempts to acquire surreptitiously the knowledge necessary to them, the author has supplied the need in this book. Drawing upon a fund of material accumulated over twenty years of work for difficult children, he gives in the form of letters to a girl on the threshold of adolescence answers to many questions which puzzle the eager minds of boys and girls. He traces the course of normal growth from birth to the age of twenty-five, and shows how the male and female elements combine to form the human personality. In a small compass he has given parents and teachers a book which will help children reach maturity ready to take an adult part in life. With this volume on their own shelves children will have no need to search the Bible for stray allusions to the act of reproduction, or borrow surreptitiously the volume on "advice to parents" supposedly kept beyond their reach.' Today it can be read in its historical context.

This book is a re-issue originally published in 1941. The language used and views portrayed are a reflection of its era and no offence is meant by the Publishers to any reader by this re-publication.

Letters to Margaret

A Simple Introduction to Psychology

Theodore Faithfull

LONDON AND NEW YORK

First published in 1941
by George Allen & Unwin Ltd

This edition first published in 2025 by Routledge
4 Park Square, Milton Park, Abingdon, Oxon, OX14 4RN

and by Routledge
605 Third Avenue, New York, NY 10017

Routledge is an imprint of the Taylor & Francis Group, an informa business

© 1941 Theodore Faithfull

All rights reserved. No part of this book may be reprinted or reproduced or utilised in any form or by any electronic, mechanical, or other means, now known or hereafter invented, including photocopying and recording, or in any information storage or retrieval system, without permission in writing from the publishers.

Publisher's Note
The publisher has gone to great lengths to ensure the quality of this reprint but points out that some imperfections in the original copies may be apparent.

Disclaimer
The publisher has made every effort to trace copyright holders and welcomes correspondence from those they have been unable to contact.

A Library of Congress record exists under LCCN: a 42000318

ISBN: 978-1-032-94619-1 (hbk)
ISBN: 978-1-003-57171-1 (ebk)
ISBN: 978-1-032-94622-1 (pbk)

Book DOI 10.4324/9781003571711

Photo Swaine

Theodore Faithfull

LETTERS TO MARGARET

A Simple Introduction to
Psychology

by

THEODORE FAITHFULL
*Formerly Principal of the Priory
Gate School*

LONDON
George Allen & Unwin Ltd

FIRST PUBLISHED IN 1941

ALL RIGHTS RESERVED

PRINTED IN GREAT BRITAIN
In 12-Point Perpetua Type
BY UNWIN BROTHERS LIMITED
WOKING

*To the children of the
Age of Conscious Understanding*

In the beginning was the Logos
(wisdom—understanding—knowledge)
and the Logos was with God and
the Logos was God . .

PREFACE

THESE letters were primarily planned for the assistance of a girl who was at that time in her twelfth year, later they went out to both boys and girls of approximately the same age. It is not every child whose parents are enlightened enough to seek psychological help for their children before the age of puberty. Many are in blind ignorance of the problems of growth which are occupying much of the time and mental energy of their son or daughter who with a little understanding help might be enjoying their school work or sleeping through nights undisturbed by mental conflicts. In book form the letters will, I hope, assist many children to traverse the difficult years of adolescence and reach manhood and womanhood without having to carry the burden of troubles which so often lead to breakdown before the middle milestone along the road of life has been reached.

One of the worst difficulties of childhood is the idea that we are different from others. When we learn that others as reticent as ourselves experience the same physical and emotional reactions, we shed, as did Christian, an intolerable burden. The other great difficulty is the criticisms bestowed upon us. Our own criticisms as we follow each step of man's evolution is more than enough without our having to accept extraneous values beyond our conception. Whatever is is true and as adults we have no right to label what we find in children "good" or "bad"; an excessive overbalance is most easily rectified by development of its reverse. It is as true now as it was two thousand years ago that without accepting our life as instinctively as a child we cannot be reborn.

"In very truth I say unto you, whosoever shall not receive the kingdom of God as a little child shall in no wise enter therein."

Many who read the letters for the first time may forcefully disclaim experience of some of the stages of normal growth I have described. "I have never bitten anyone; never had a desire to destroy an animal or poison my relatives; have never cried myself to sleep or known an hour of fear or anxiety."

Thousands who so disclaim may or may not be deluding themselves but they would do well to bear in mind that the intensity of their emotional disturbance is a fairly accurate measure of repression. We have a very convenient way of forgetting the happenings in one stage of our life when we pass into a new one, though to be free from the unconscious effect of these repressions, they must ultimately be brought into relation with the experiences of to-day. Few who have pursued the road of self-analysis have not been

Spiritual Alchemy

Illustration from *Twelve Keys of Philosophy*, attributed to Brother Basilius Valentinus. Paris, 1660. Reproduced from the copy in the British Museum

astonished when they have unearthed experiences that they have at one stage or another pushed into oblivion. That some people have been so frustrated in early life that all their experiences have been one-sided is a regrettable truth. These people will in making their denials be expressing literal truth. For many such the normal, though primitive, experiences of early childhood have never come to the surface to demand expression. The earlier in life that they can be released so much the less will be the wasted opportunities for appreciation and experience of the higher mental activities.

The unknown author of that wonderful epic poem the Book of Job described the re-education of the apparently successful man of the world and his journey along the road to understanding through suffering. It will be more fully understood if studied with the aid of William Blake's illustrations and Joseph Wicksteed's explanations of Blake's work. To the present age psychology is offering the way of self analysis and synthesis as a road to spiritual unity. My experience in recent years makes it certain beyond all reasonable doubt, that in addition to the many children and adolescents who will find help in these simple expositions of the steps of the ladder of life, there are many adults who will find in them explanations of mental worries that are driving them to physical or mental breakdown Many who have broken down and are perhaps passing through months of depression or infantile delusions of their self-importance and omnipotence and who in so doing are retracing their steps to childhood or infancy to find their other self, will with their help make the journey with greater content and the confidence of an ultimate return to normality enriched by their experiences.

In the course of my professional work I some years ago had occasion to help a young woman who had over-developed the objective male side of her personality and had returned to infancy to find the emotional and reproductive female self. The strait-jacket and other indignities which she had experienced because of her desire to feed herself with her hands and walk about free from clothing had nearly broken her will to return to normality. The information contained in these letters enabled her to récover her balance and in process of time to reach full physical maturity.

Only recently another confidante, narrating her experiences during an unnecessarily long period of depression, described how she felt entirely out of touch with those around her. Surrounded with loving care, she was hardly better off than the inmate of the mental hospital I have just mentioned. This woman, taken for the purpose of diversion to the pictures, was unaware of any other reaction than intense skin irritations which often enough compelled her to leave the theatre. The pictures meant no more to her than to a one-year-old child, whose means of self-expression she did in fact use.

There is one criticism I would wish to forestall, and that is the inevitable one that more harm than good can be done by bringing the facts of growth and life to consciousness. The day-to-day study of the delinquencies dealt with in our police courts, the problems with which our coroners' courts have to deal and the criminal actions which occupy the time of the judges in the High Courts are all in my opinion evidence to the contrary. Everyone who reads a newspaper however perfunctorily must be aware of the appalling waste of human life through ignorance. Nor is the trouble confined to the social strata which is supposed to produce criminals.

The human race is entering upon a new phase of consciousness. Our appreciation of poetry and religious symbolism will be none the less enthralling because we are able to trace, through each successive stage, the earlier means by which the basic male and female elements which go to build up the individual personality have found expression.

Only through the balance within ourselves of these opposing forces can we find the unity which is the true Kingdom of Heaven.

THEODORE FAITHFULL

BIRMINGHAM *1941*

I

MY DEAR MARGARET,

If you have not already done so I want you to read a simple book about life; the one I suggest is *Life, How It Comes*, by Dr. Reid Heyman. If you have not read a biological book you will find in this one many things of interest about life in animals. I shall assume in these letters that you have read and digested this book or some book of a similar character.

When we are born we have in us an immense fund of knowledge, all the important experiences of man in process of his evolution from the single-celled protozoon to the fully developed civilized man of the present day. In spite of having all that knowledge it is great fun linking up what we know, buried in memory with what we can experience in the world around us and so bringing what we know to consciousness. I will give you a simple example: A baby a few months old knows what we mean by biting. Millions of its human and animal ancestors have used their teeth for getting food and for breaking it up before swallowing it, but as a tiny baby he can only press his gums upon the nipples of his mother's breasts or upon a finger or any other solid object on which he wishes to assert himself. A few months later he will know in another way, because as soon as he has cut his teeth the knowledge in him is linked with the experience of biting an apple or a biscuit. He will then be just as busy trying to bring into the reality of to-day some other memory-born racial experience. The Greeks had a word for this inner knowledge. It was the word Logos and we have used it to build up many of our names for different branches of knowledge. The book you have been reading was on what is called Bio-logy or the knowledge of life, but you would have brought very little of your inner knowledge to the surface of your mind if you stopped your enquiries there. In these letters I want to tell you something about Psycho-logy, that is, the knowledge about the psyche, the mind or soul, that part of living things which cannot be appreciated by the five senses but which, in spite of that, is a very real part of us, a part which often uses the five senses as a means of expression and a means of making contacts with other people. It is necessary for us to make contacts because isolation brings us to death, while happy contacts give us ever renewed life. When you press the button of an electric bell or turn the switch of an electric light circuit the current flows and the bell rings or the lamp lights up, so it is with the flow of psychic energy from person to person and from people to animals. Some people think also that there is a flow from vegetation, trees, grass and bushes, and use this to

LETTERS TO MARGARET

explain the invigorating effect of going into the fields and woods in spring when everything around is bursting with new life.

In another letter I shall refer to psychic energy as "libido," which is the modern psychological term. As in the years to come your reading widens you will find this energy mentioned under many names in the languages of every civilization of which there is record. We use it in our growth, our games, our singing, our dreaming and our thinking, in fact, in all those things which entitle us to say that we are "alive" in the animal and human sense and not just existing.

At one time people thought that Bio-logy and Psycho-logy were quite separate subjects, that we could say this thing is of the "body" and this of the "soul," but in recent years learned men have come to see the truth that poets have always known, that the two things body and soul are so closely bound together in life that it is not possible to separate them. If your biological memory was not closely interwoven in the cells from which as you know our bodies are made up, you would not have known what size or shape to build different parts of your body so that you could come out of your mother a perfect baby nor would you develop each part of your body as the baby develops its teeth to serve your needs as you grow to maturity.

For this reason when writing to you these letters

about psychology I shall be constantly referring to what are strictly speaking Biological subjects. The study of life is in fact a blend of Bio-logy and Psycho-logy, so my letters will really be about Biopsycho-logy, but that is too big a mouthful for everyday use! As long as we both know that by "psychology" I mean "life" you won't have to bother your head about what are really futile divisions of the one subject which has always been of interest to civilized men.

In the study of Biology you must have noticed with interest that the most primitive animals are not divided into male and female, though some of them have gone half way, as, for example, the earth-worm and the snail, and are at one time male and another female according to the season of the year, and that the male cells of these animals are not used to fertilize the egg cells of the same animal but are exchanged with another animal of the same kind to bring about what is called cross-fertilization. All the higher animals are differentiated into male and female. To get from the first a real undestanding of psychology you must get it clear in your mind that though our bodies and those of birds, reptiles and mammals are divided in this way for the purpose of what is called procreation, each one of us has a complete psyche. Every girl child carries all the memories of the males who have been her ancestors, and every boy child has the inner knowledge of the functions which can only be brought into the reality of experience by females.

You will have learned that the egg is large, slow-moving, placid, receptive, conservative (in the sense of storing up), it is also self-sacrificing, as part of the process of creation, and can be said to enjoy the pleasure of pain; and that the male fertilizing cell or sperm is tiny, active, impetuous, outgoing, dominating; it can be said to be cruel in its possessiveness but self-sacrificing in that it expends itself in enabling that which attracts it to create new life. These two cells show in miniature all the many expressions of life which can be called truly male and female.

As I go on with the story of *Life, How it Develops* I shall have again and again to refer to the male or female expression of the same thing, and it will make things clearer for you if I use two biological signs, the first ♀ gives the information that the thing referred to is female, and ♂ that the thing is male. In my next letter I will tell you something about love, not the act of reproduction which can be an act of love, but is not necessarily so, but the wider psychological love, and in that letter I shall have to describe love ♂ and love ♀ as two things as widely different as the egg and the sperm cell, which as you know, join to make every new life in the higher animals and plants, and some of the more highly differentiated single-celled organisms.

Your affectionate friend

II

MY DEAR MARGARET,

A very wonderful essay on love was written by Plato, a Greek Philosopher who lived from *c.* 428 to 348 B.C. The essay is in the form of a dialogue and is called "The Banquet." You will enjoy reading it when you are a little older, and each time afterwards that you read it again you will learn more from it. In it one thing stands out very clearly and is expressed in different ways by those whom Plato describes as taking part in the debate, and that is the truth that Love has two opposite poles, or, as an English translation has it: "a totally opposite nature." Further, you will learn from it that love in each of its forms is the outcome of a desire for happiness and is obtained as a result of the willing flow of psychic energy from one person to another. At one point when Plato makes Socrates say what he had learned from Diotema the prophetess, he names the two sides of love Poverty ($♀$) and Plenty ($♂$). You will notice that after "Poverty" and "Plenty" I have put the two signs I mentioned in my first letter. I will give you a simple illustration to make the meaning of the names clearer. If you have a glass of water and an empty glass the first could symbolize $♂$ love and the empty one $♀$ love.

LETTERS TO MARGARET

Unified love would be achieved when you tilted one glass towards the other and there was a flow from one glass to the other. If you covered up the mouths of the glasses each form would be inactive and so they would remain until the covers were removed and the contents could flow freely to and fro.

Have you yet come across the *Songs of Innocence* and *The Songs of Experience*, by our greatest English poet William Blake? Blake was a man whose inner knowledge of life, that is, of psychology, was profound, and like all real poets he said much more in his songs than on the surface the words convey. Here is *The Clod and the Pebble*:

> "Love seeketh not itself to please,
> Nor for itself has any care,
> But for another gives its ease
> And builds a Heaven in Hell's despair."
>
> So sung a little clod of clay,
> Trodden with the cattle's feet,
> But a pebble of the brook
> Warbled out these metres meet:
>
> "Love seeketh only self to please,
> To bind another in its delight,
> Joys in another's loss of ease
> And builds a Hell in Heaven's despite."

The "clod of clay" is describing the ♀ love, "The

pebble of the brook" the ♂ love. The clod of clay is the form love must take in the poet, the inventor, the story-teller, in fact in the creative artist whatever form he may use for the expression of his thoughts. It is also the form which love must be shown in a woman towards her husband if she is to find happiness in her home and children. "The pebble in the brook" is the other form of love which pours itself out upon the object it seeks to bind, not necessarily as Blake seems to suggest here, entirely selfishly, but because he expects the object loved to produce something worth while out of the flow of energy which has taken place.

This brings me to two more words which you will have to learn if you are going to get these things clear: they are subjective and objective. These two words are not only expressive of the two forms of love but express also very clearly the real maleness and femaleness in its many forms that you will discover in yourself and in those around you. I will imagine a situation which will serve as an explanation for you. When you hit a tennis ball you are being objective to it, but if the boy or girl you are playing against drives the ball so that it hits you in the eye your experience of the ball and of pain is subjective. If you lose your temper and shout out "You beast, I hate you" and fling your racquet at the net, you are behaving objectively, as a result of the pain. That is to say, you are behaving in a ♂ way, but if you collapse on to the ground and burst into sobs and tears, you are reacting subjectively, i.e. in a ♀ way. To take the supposed incident a step further, if Mother comes out and excitedly fusses over you she is behaving objectively. If your friend is feeling so sympathetic that she cannot eat any tea, she is also reacting subjectively to what we will assume was an unfortunate accident. On the other hand, if she says "It was all your fault, Margaret, you shouldn't have let it hit you," she will also be acting objectively to the accident, and will have no difficulty in eating as good a tea as she usually does.

The proportion of our available psychic energy we use subjectively or objectively varies enormously in different people. In others it varies at different stages in their development. I shall have much more to tell you about that in later letters.

You will discover in time that life is easier for girls who have a definite balance towards subjectivity as this enables them to accept motherhood, and all it entails. Equally, the boy with a definite balance towards objectivity, finds life easier on the whole than the dreamy subjective boy. In the depth of our inner selves, however, we all want to experience all life in its two forms, and some people have to wait until well after middle age before they can do so to their satisfaction. Have you ever seen people dress up with masks on the back of their heads? Members of a concert party will sometimes sing part of a song facing the audience, then suddenly they all turn round and appear as quite different people. Such a piece of entertainment expresses a real truth, but many people are quite frightened by their other self, especially if it has the appearance of being much younger than the side they are used to.

Jesus of Nazareth, whose teachings formed the basis of the Christian religion, explained to his followers many truths by means of parables. He told one parable which shows the difference between the objective and the subjective man's reaction to a new idea. Here it is, taken from the Authorized Version:

"A certain man had two sons; and he came to the first and said, Son, go work to-day in my vineyard. He answered and said, I will not; but afterwards he repented and went. And he came to the second and said likewise. And he answered and said, I go, sir; and went not."

The first type of person dislikes any new idea but falls into line when his barrier is down and is very tenacious of anything once it is an established habit of thought or action. The second type is the "yes-man" in the language of to-day, but they subjectively think things over and they often ultimately decide on a different line of action than their apparent willingness to agree indicates. It is again the question of the use to which the psychic energy is put. The objective—♂ attitude man is the resistive type and the yes-man is the subjective ♀ type. I will tell you more about this psychic energy, or as it is now often called libido, in my next letter.

Your affectionate friend

III

MY DEAR MARGARET,

In my last letter I began to tell you something about the different kinds of love. You can call them Mummy love (♀) and Daddy love (♂), if you like, if you remember that Mummy can also love in the ♂ way and Daddy in the ♀ way. It is true to say that very many men of those who are really grown up have more of the ♀ love in them than most women, and many women are very rich in ♂ love. It is all-important to our happiness what part of ourselves we satisfy with each of the two forms.

I promised to tell you more about the psychic energy or libido, as all my later letters will have to do with the different ways we use it in order to be happy. Here again it is the direction of flow which decides for us whether the energy is being used in a male or female way. Have you ever tried the game of staring someone down? I can remember playing it in my early school days. The two people playing the game stare into each other's eyes until one has to look away. The one who looks away first loses the game. Psychologists are inventing many gadgets for the purpose of testing the objective and subjective reactions in people, but that is a simple and when first used an accurate test. No machine can yet test the quantity of libido, but some people, as you know, make their presence felt instantly when joining a party of friends. Others can arrive on the scene and be unnoticed. Others instead of bringing life into a group have always what is called a wet blanket effect. Another rather interesting and amusing way of noting the ♀ and ♂ direction of flow is to read someone else's paper in a bus or a train. It is best to choose someone sitting opposite to you. If you direct your flow in an outward way, staring at the print the man or woman behind the paper almost immediately becomes fidgety, crosses or uncrosses his legs, coughs, or perhaps looks over his paper and glares at you. If instead of flowing outwardly you hold your energy and quietly focus your eyes so as to allow the print to become legible, you can read down a long paragraph and cause no discomfort to the owner of the paper.

The outward flow of libido whether from skin surface, the eyes or other specialized organs is the ♂ form. The pleasure of "Looking" is one of the established ways of getting happiness. Do you know *New Sights*, by Edith King?—

> "I like to see a thing I know
> Has not been seen before,
> That's why I cut my apple through
> To look into the core.

> It's nice to think though many an eye
>   Has seen the ruddy skin,
> Mine is the very first to spy
>   The five brown pips within."

Those few lines express the pleasure in a very delightful way. Everyone who is not blind uses his or her eyes for getting happiness in this way. Blind people seem to be able to increase the "looking" power of the cells over the whole surface of their bodies. Babies have extraordinarily sensitive skin cells but people who can see with their eyes lose to a great extent this power as their eyesight develops, people blind from birth never lose it and those who become blind later in life regain the faculty. I shall have more to tell you later about the pleasure of looking and the pleasure of being looked at. Perhaps as I have said something about one of the five senses, you will like me to point out to you some interesting facts about the others. They are, you know, hearing, tasting, touching and smelling. Tasting is a channel of perception of which we make great use in our early years. As soon as a baby is capable of grasping anything he will try to bring the object to the mouth so that he can taste it. In later life the habit remains as a means of exercising a choice of food. If the word is enlarged to take in the acts of sucking and biting it has the same duality as I explained to you we have in the use of the eyes. The *sucking* of sweets, the *biting* of chewing gum, or the ends of pens and pencils, the biting of those they feel are their enemies, are quite common reactions in small children. It dies out as a means of satisfaction but the pleasure-giving habit of kissing remains throughout our lives. One little boy of my acquaintance used to ask his friends "May I taste you?" when he wanted to express his love for them with a kiss.

Civilized people have to a large extent lost the sense of smell but many people react with pleasure to the scent of certain flowers and of many herbs, the smell of soil after a shower, of new-mown hay, of horses and their stables, whilst other smells are obnoxious to most people, as, for instance, that given out from the excrement of cats.

The smell of people varies greatly; the smell of one person's hair may be almost intoxicatingly delightful to one acquaintance and distasteful to another. Here again we find a duality––not only is smelling used as a means of perception but the giving out of smells can be a positive objective act. Some animals and plants defend themselves by throwing out smells unpleasant to their enemies. Human beings also change the odour of their bodies to keep at bay those they dislike and attract those they love, or if owing to over-civilization they have temporarily lost the power they consciously cover themselves with the concentrated odour of flowers or make their rooms attractive with flowers of sweet-smelling flowering plants.

Our fourth sense, hearing, has also lost some of its acuteness among civilized races but some people have a very wide range of sound perception or as we say, have a "delicate ear." Some small children are very sensitive to sound and it is certain that we use this sense organ even before birth. Loud noises from the outer world reach us through the walls of our mother's body and the gurgling noises of the food passing through our mother's intestine give us early and pleasing memories of running water. One of my sons remembered hearing the doctor say "Boy" the moment after his birth, though he described it as something that had happened in a dream. It is the delicacy of our hearing apparatus which has given us language and, of course, all the subtle delights of music. Hearing itself or rather the ears have not the power of outward expression, but their opposite is the sound box in our windpipe by which we are able to express not only variation in the volume of vibrations which are heard by the ears as noise but are also able to express ourselves emotionally, arousing in other persons fear, desire for love or a display of violence in some form according to the physical and psychological make up of our hearers.

The last and fifth sense is the sense of touch. It is used far more than you might at first thought suppose to be the case and would be used much more if we weren't so constantly wrapped up in clothes. You will remember how in your biology book the amoeba was described as being very sensitive to touch. Without any specialized sense organs it directs its activities in this or that direction, chooses and refuses food material in its path of progress. I have already told you that a baby is very sensitive all over its skin surface. Most babies are generally quick to show with whom they enjoy physical contact. When suckling his mother, a baby senses the contact with her body it experienced for nine months before birth and the wise mother, if from some mishap she is not able to feed her child from her breasts, will give it "a holding" after each bottle.

A tired child will often come to those it loves for "a holding." Later in life some areas of the body become more sensitive both for reception and expression than others but at least one of the pleasures of dancing lies in the opportunity of close physical contact. Children and lovers hold hands and use the contact to establish a flow of psychic energy from one to the other. A flow can also be established between human beings and animals, as, for instance, a horse and its rider. It would be interesting for you to note whether you play the male to your ponies, flowing to them in an attempt to dominate them or take from them, calling them into a lively and co-operative activity. One of the most famous horse breakers of the last century, a man named Rarey, had the latter power to so great an extent that the most violent horse would become gentle in his hands. Recently I travelled in a carriage where a very male little boy of about three was also travelling with his parents. I noticed when he wished to make friends with anyone he hit them. The father did not recognize the action as an offer of friendship and tried to stop him, but the action was a natural one. I accepted his offer of friendship and he was soon occupied with looking at the pictures in the book I was reading. Many people establish a flow through touch with their pets, dogs, cats, or rabbits, but it is not an entirely healthy practice any more then it is wise for adults to use children for getting satisfaction which it would be more normal to obtain from an adult friendship.

We extend and develop the power of touching by means of many inventions; needles, knives and forks and many other things are gadgets to extend and concentrate what are called our tactile powers. The expert pianist is able to develop the tactile sense to produce a wide range of sounds which can be perceived not only by the ears but the skin cells of those within range of the sound waves.

Finally to close this long letter I would remind you that the "laying on of hands" has been used in many religions as a means of healing. By its means a sick person's cells are often encouraged to recommence activity. A gifted masseur gives more than mere mechanical movement to the muscles he or she manipulates. In the Roman and Anglican Churches the hands of the bishop are placed upon the head of each child at the time he or she is admitted to full church membership.

      Your affectionate friend

IV

MY DEAR MARGARET,

You tell me in your letter that you would like a book from which you could learn more about people. I think you would enjoy reading *How you are Made*, by Amabel Williams-Ellis. When you have read that, it will be easier for you to follow what I will tell you about the different stages in our lives between the time we are born and what is called maturity or being "grown up."

In this letter I want to tell you something about what is sometimes called the sixth sense, or the intuition. We use it far more than most people are aware. It is markedly in evidence between mothers and their very young children but we do not find our own feet until the link has been broken. It comes into use again whenever there is a strong love or friendship between two people and is used where intimate groups of people are formed, as, for instance, a school team, or a body of people who meet to take part in religious services. It can be used both for good and evil by orators who have the power of stirring up crowds or can show itself spontaneously at periods of great emotion as, for instance, a coronation or an outbreak of war.

LETTERS TO MARGARET

When we are young we by its use feel ourselves very much part of nature, some of course more than others. This was especially true of the English poet of nature, William Wordsworth. Some people think he never grew into the imaginative level, which we enter, as I shall tell you in a later letter, in early adolescence, but expressed in his poetry that which he experienced, through his exceptional powers of sensing and feeling. Here are three stanzas from a poem he named *To my Sister*, written in the spring of 1798:

> "There is a blessing in the air,
>   Which seems a sense of joy to yield
> To the bare trees and mountains bare,
>   And grass in the green field.
>
> Love, now a universal birth,
>   From heart to heart is stealing,
> From earth to man, from man to earth
>   It is the hour of feeling.
>
> One moment now may give us more
>   Than years of toiling reason:
> Our minds shall drink at every pore
>   The spirit of the season."

The word "intuition" means "taught inside," that is, taught by other means than the five senses. We may get the information from the past experiences of the race, in the same way that we inherit instincts, from experiences in infancy and early childhood before we came to consciousness of ourselves, from the unconscious mental activity of those around us, or from conscious experiences which we have or think we have forgotten.

The five senses about which I wrote you in my last letter are all concerned with what are called reality or material things. These things bear relation to time and measurement but the sixth sense can ignore time. For example, a man of sixty can in a fraction of an instant re-live the experience of being a small child digging in the sand. A girl child may know in advance of time the size of her family that is to be or a man dream of a powerful emotional experience years before it has taken place. It is used by water diviners and by fortune tellers though it is probable that those possessed with what is called second sight cannot distinguish wishes in the minds of their questioners from the events of which there is evidence in the questioner's mind in advance of time, a factor which makes the soothsayer a somewhat unreliable guide.

When I was a boy a new star was discovered and the astronomers decided that it must have been formed before the time of Jesus Christ, say over two thousand years ago. Now light travels at roughly 300,000 kilometres a second! That thought brought it home to me that space and measurement do not really exist apart from ourselves and our immediate environment.

LETTERS TO MARGARET

Space must go on for ever. In the same way we can say time has no limits and is only the human way of spacing events or happenings in our world and neighbouring planets. Have you read Van Loon's *The Story of Mankind*? If you have you will remember the Norse Tale of the great rock visited every thousand years by a bird who sharpens his beak upon it. It is said that when the rock is worn away one moment of time will have passed. Time then is as measureless as space.

I have told you that a mother is closely connected with her child by means of this sixth sense. This is the case to such an extent that the first child feels at once when the mother has a new child within her body and will show it in numerous ways, such as thumb sucking, wetting its bed at night, or showing antagonism to the mother. If a mother at night turns her love towards the father the child in a cot in the next room will often wake and call the mother to her.

We all have to be weaned from feeding from the mother's breasts and before three years old we ought also to be weaned from this close psychic association, otherwise whenever the mother lets her interest go to friends we tumble down or otherwise hurt ourselves, a thing we would never think of doing if we had been weaned and were living our own lives in temporary association with playmates or any friendly human being or animal who happened to be about.

You will learn from the biology books how a baby gets its nourishment when inside its mother and how the cord through which the blood circulates is broken at birth. Though this cord must be broken for all, many children, especially when families are small, never break the psychic cord. There are many apparently grown-up people who are tied in this way to their mothers. Should they marry, which many of them do not do, the attachment spells unhappiness for the husband or wife and the whole new family.

Sometimes the association of one person with another through the sixth sense is so strong the one will answer the thought of the other before it has become a question. The relationship may be a very equal and balanced one, or it may be that one person may play the dominant ♂ role and the other the receptive ♀ role. One being always the transmitter, to use a term used by electrical engineers, and the other a receiver. This thought transference is called telepathy. You will find two good examples of it in *With Mystics and Magicians in Tibet*, by Madame Alexandra David Neal.*

If the mother or father of a family is a very powerful transmitter, ♂, he or she fills the mind of the children with suggestions as to what hurts and what doesn't hurt and what is "right" and what is "wrong," so that the child receiver is in a sorely puzzled state as

* See Appendix I.

to whether to believe her own developing urges are right or the grown-up's ideas which he or she has not been able to resist. I remember one family where it was the nurse who was such a powerful transmitter ♂ that she was causing one child to stammer and one to wet its bed.

It is possible to test the use of the sixth sense in many ways. Some years ago while I was walking up Regent Street not far from Piccadilly Circus, I began talking to the friend walking with me about someone I had not seen or thought about for some years. Before we reached Oxford Street I met this person, a fairly clear example of sensing an experience in advance of time.

On another occasion I was walking in the garden of an empty house and let myself get away from the present by a sort of relaxation. I then asked myself "shall I live here?", the reply came immediately "Yes, but not now." I decided on another house which was more convenient for a school and had a river running beside the garden deep enough for swimming. Three months later owing to a kink in the landlord's mind about co-education I was refused the lease of the house near the river and moved to the other house which was still empty.

If you write a letter to an intimate friend, that is, someone whom you love, and are feeling very miserable, you cannot hide your feelings by writing an apparently cheerful letter. When your friend receives it, even if it is months later during which it has gone half-way round the world, the time, so to speak, dissolves and the reader is with you at the time of your writing the letter and feels the emotion you strove so hard to repress, or if you are writing letters of invitation to a party and you say "I don't like so and so and don't want to ask her," and then because mother thinks you ought to, you write a nice letter saying how pleased you will be to see her, it is more than probable that the child who gets the invitation will say at once "I don't want to go." Her mother may say "it's such a nice letter and they have such a nice garden," but these arguments mean nothing; the child you have written to feels you don't like her and ten to one if she writes and accepts she will have a headache when the party day comes and will in that way give herself a real excuse to stop away.

Sometimes when owing to illness we are denied expression of our energy in normal ways, we show excessive development of one faculty. Recently a boy of seventeen years died suddenly who had for years made use of the sixth sense for earning his living on the stage. His eyes were covered with dough and then bandaged, but he could still tell what had been written on a blackboard. It is not known whether his power was due to a telepathic relationship with his father or if he had the power of sight which did not need eyes for the purpose of perception, but there can be no doubt that he was using a power which in a much less developed form is an attribute of every human being.

The use of the sixth sense or the intuition on the imaginative level is more often apparent in women than in men. It is an objective ♂ attribute and as I shall show you later corresponds with the creative ♀ imagination of men. Some doctors have made use of the women gifted in this way to find out what part of the body of a patient is unhealthy. Men and women psychologists use it, though often unconsciously, to bring to light forgotten troubles in those who come to them for help.

In recent years scientists have given to the unconscious mind very much laborious study. So much has been learned that many people are joining the great religious teachers of the world who have always held that the *real* is the unseen and the unreal what we can sense with the five senses. One man's thought may permeate a world of human beings far beyond his range of personal knowledge, or as Tennyson puts it:—

"More things are wrought by prayer than this world dreams of."

Some day you may be interested in the study of what has been named Metapsychics.

Your affectionate friend

V

MY DEAR MARGARET,

You ask me to make the difference between real and unreal clearer to you, so before I go on to something fresh, I must try what I can do about it. I wonder if you keep a diary, because there are two ways of keeping one. The first way is to be very careful about dates; it reads something like this:

Feb. 1st. Got up late. Strawberry jam for tea.
Feb. 2nd. Rained all day. No games so read *Robbery under Arms* after school.
Feb. 3rd. Bought a packet of 100 stamps, 6d., and some seeds for my garden, 4d.
Feb. 4th.
Feb. 5th. Auntie Floss came to stay. Took me to the pictures, saw . . . .
Feb. 6th. Played against the upper fourth, our side won.

The other kind is often written in a plain book and the dates are put in in ink or pencil and reads more like this:—

Feb. 1st. When I came home to-day, I found Bonzo had chewed my fountain pen. Felt I hated him. It's funny that I can love and hate the same thing.

Feb. 4th. (Copy of a poem the diarist has read and liked.)

Feb. 6th. When Auntie Floss was playing the piano today I forgot what room I was in. It seemed as if we were by the sea, the sun was shining, etc.

Feb. 10th. I dreamed . . . . (Then there is almost a page of dream.)

Feb. 20th. Daddy has been home for four days' leave. We've done lots of things but I don't remember what. But it has been lovely. Mother has been singing, I think Daddy must make her very happy. . . . I shall have lots of children when I grow up.

Which diary deals with real things? The first is a list of facts, the second is a record of thoughts.

In my first two letters I reminded you about what you had learnt in the Biology book, about the beginning of life. How we and most animals and plants start on our life by the fusing of two independent cells, the ovum and the spermatozoon. So different in character are these cells that they can be taken to represent all the opposing groups of characteristics which can be discovered in every human personality.

I used these cells to illustrate the difference between the two kinds of love, the male ($♂$) love, the giving out form, and the female ($♀$), the receiving form, but all our other attributes are found to have opposites. For example, tears and anger are opposites, and the pleasure in being hurt is the opposite of the pleasure from hurting others or in destroying objects. If you care to do a bit of thinking you can find in yourself opposites for nearly everything. It would be quite justifiable to coin two new words for them and call one group ovic and the other spermic according to whether they belonged more to the receptive, absorbing, creative characteristics of the ovum or to the active, positive, outward turning characteristic of the sperm. Other names for the two groups are hysteric and phallic, which means possessing the characteristics which find expression in the reproductive apparatus of woman and man respectively.

In this letter I want especially to tell you about the two divisions of your psychic or spiritual self. Some day you will come across the word "ego" which is the Latin word for "I," that part of us which can consciously think about the rest.

When we are conceived, that is to say, when the sperm supplied by our father reaches and blends with the ovum detached from our mother, and we attach ourselves to our mother's womb for the purpose of nourishment and protection, we have no conscious knowledge of the "I." We feel ourselves intimately part of our surroundings and part of the main stream of life from which we came. For some time after birth we continue to be very much part of our environment but there is in all of us a "Me" and we early learn to claim a thing as "mine." For many people the first conscious memory dates about the beginning of their fourth year.

The subjective "me" can also stand aside as the "I" does later and views the physical personality as something apart. Several children and adults have told me of things they thought they had watched happening to others when they were small, which quite certainly happened to themselves. One lady described how she saw a little girl placed on a table after her bath with something wrapped round her, she then saw her tumble off the table, the door open and a man rush in and pick her up. The little girl was herself about the age of two and a half and the man was her father. Other people describe such events as happening in dreams.

Though in the early months of life within our mothers there is no "I" and no "Me," there is every reason to believe that there is a non-material part of us which carries the ancestral memories and which directs our growth. In recent years this part of us has been given the name of "It." Later in life when we can recognize the "Me" and the "I" division the "It" part has still a lot to do; it is always building and rebuilding the body, directing the manufacture of the digestive juices, and the provision of the energy for the use of the "Me" and the "I."

Many religions of which there is record in the

history of man, have shown the importance of the three divisions of ourselves by means of a triangle △ —the male self, the female self and the spirit which operates in both. Before I have finished these letters I may send you one showing how the importance of these divisions becomes less as we grow older, and that eventually they blend to form a complete personality sometimes expressed by the four-sided figure the square □ . But to return to the "I" or ego, in a book by Richard Hughes called *High Wind in Jamaica*, there is a description of a little girl of $10\frac{1}{2}$ becoming aware of herself and realizing for the first time that she had an "I" which could direct her actions. Here are a few paragraphs I have copied out for you——

"And then an event did occur to Emily, of considerable importance. She suddenly realized who she was.

There is little reason that one can see why it should not have happened to her five years earlier, or even five years later; and none why it should have come that particular afternoon.

She had been playing houses in a nook right in the bows, behind the windlass (on which she had hung a devil's claw as a door knocker), and tiring of it was walking rather aimlessly aft, thinking vaguely about some bees and a fairy queen, when it suddenly flashed into her mind that she was *she*.

She stopped dead and began looking all over her person which came within the range of her eyes. She could not see much, except a foreshortened view of the front of her frock, and her hands when she lifted them for inspection: but it was enough for her to form a rough idea of the little body she suddenly realized to be hers.

She began to laugh rather mockingly. Well, she thought in effect: 'Fancy you of all people, going and getting caught like this!—You can't get out of it now, not for a very long time: you'll have to go through with being a child, and growing up, and getting old, before you will be quit of this mad prank!'

Determined to avoid any interruption of this highly important occasion she began to climb the ratlines, on her way to her favourite perch at the mast head. Each time she moved an arm or a leg in this simple action, however, it struck her with fresh amusement to find them obeying her so readily. Memory told her, of course, that they had always done so before: but before, she had never realized how surprising this was.

Once settled on her perch, she began examining the skin of her hands with the utmost care: for it was hers. She slipped a shoulder out of the top of her frock; and having peeped in to make sure that she really was continuous under her clothes, she shrugged it up to touch her cheek. The contact of her face and the warm bare hollow of her shoulder gave her a comfortable thrill, as if it was the caress of some kind friend. But whether the feeling came to her through her cheek or her shoulder, which was the caresser and which the caressed, that no analysis could tell her."

Some people grow the male and female sides of themselves pretty nearly equally. Other people leave part of themselves anchored and have to go back and find that part later in life if they are to reach what is called maturity.

You, for instance, at the age of eleven might be as much boy as girl or shall I say as much grown up on the "I" side as the "Me" side (Fig. *a*) or you might be made up of an eleven-years-old boy and a three-years-old girl (*b*), or of course it might be the other way round, an eleven-years-old girl and a three-years-old boy (*c*), or even younger (*d*) (*e*). The side which wants to work and play objectively would then be grown more than the female side which might find expression in anxiety and tears or even, if under three years, as it does in some boys and girls, in wetting their knickers or wetting their beds at night. If the girl side of a child of eleven years is his or her birthday age and the boy side left anchored in the past, the boy side may seek for satisfaction in

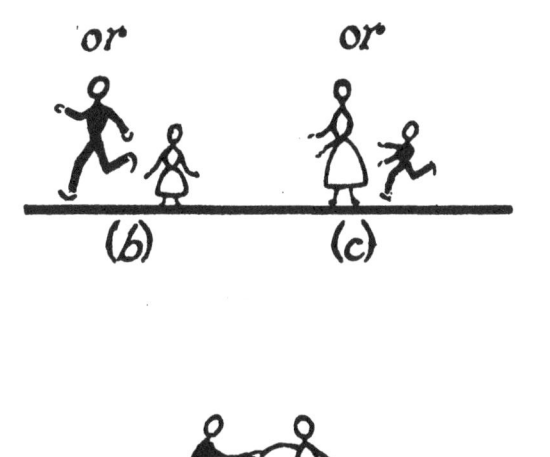

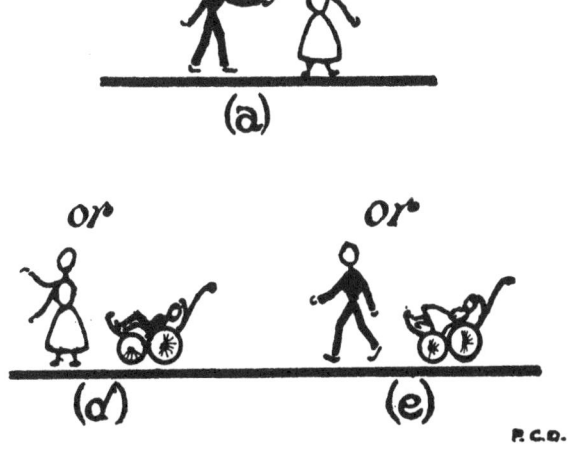

DIAGRAMMATIC SKETCH TO SHEW FIXATION OR ANCHORING
OF ONE SIDE OF THE PERSONALITY

outbursts of anger or in cruelty such as teasing other children.

It is not of course our fault if we do not grow our dual selves equally up to ten or eleven, it is largely a question of environment, how much we have been left alone, or to what extent we have had to be part of the lives of the grown-up people around us.

Sometimes after anchoring one side, the "It" starts it growing again later, leaving an unfilled gap in our experiences. That gives us uncomfortable feelings of something missing. It is however possible for us to pull up our anchors later in life and to grow up that side of us which has failed to mature or to fill the gap or gaps which have been left. The case occurs to me of a young man who had grown almost exclusively along the female or "Me" side and then at about fifteen years swung over to the objective male side. He had to go back to babyhood and slowly grow up the boy side.

I mentioned earlier in this letter that human beings have built up religions which help them to mature two sides and to find the oneness they are seeking. In adolescence we reach that stage in our individual lives at which the human race began to feel this need, then we in our turn seek an understanding through symbols.

If you have grasped the simple truth that there are two sides of your spiritual or psychological self you will follow more easily the letters in which I am going to tell you first about the stages of growth from your birthday to the end of the female pubertal period, which is normally for a girl in the twelfth or thirteenth year, and then on to psychological maturity at the end of adolescence.

Puberty is the name given to the time when the boy or girl's body is capable of use for reproduction. The male pubertal period follows the female and is completed some two years later.

Your affectionate friend

VI

MY DEAR MARGARET,

With this letter we are going back again to think about the life of a small baby, and I hope in subsequent letters to take you stage by stage through the years between your first birthday and the end of what is called adolescence, somewhere between eighteen and twenty-one years old when we begin to look really grown up. I think I told you in an earlier letter that we bring with us when we are born memories of the untold thousands of years that have measured man's progress from the single-celled animal to the kind of men and women we are now. Scientists call us *Homo Sapiens,* or the "wise man," but at times like the present when all nations are trying to settle their difficulties by destroying each other in warfare it is rather doubtful to what extent we deserve the name. These memories we have with us when the germs of human life, the egg and the sperm, contributed by our mother and father fuse to make a new person. To these memories by the time of our first birthday we have added the memories of our experiences within our mother. If our mother has been well and happy during those nine months we dream of our life in the womb as a life in a beautiful garden, but if our mother was worried or perhaps very ill for part of the time she was carrying us about with her, we bring with us memories of her unhappiness and think of the past as a dark and dismal pit which we are afraid of re-entering. Always we have the memory of running water, and when late in life we are ready to start on some new adventure we are apt to dream of swimming in the sea or being tossed about in a boat. Perhaps you have seen a reproduction of Watts's painting of a child running up a beach out of a curling wave; it is called, I think, *Whither?*

The act of being born is itself an important memory; if it was a long and difficult struggle both for one's mother and oneself, it may be a cause of fear of a lurking danger in us. But its importance as a memory to us is much less if we have a real welcome on arrival and find not only food but the security of love. When within our mothers we are most of the time huddled up with our knees to our chins, our heads upwards, then a few hours before birth we turn round ready to butt our way into the world, as soon as our mother is ready to part with us. Some children I have known, before going to sleep each night, will butt their heads against the sides of their cot or against the pillows. They are acting the experience of being born in order to help them to enter again into the forgetfulness which comes with sleep. Clowns will often get a laugh from their audiences by butting their heads on the ground, and all-powerful monarchs in the East have expected their vassals to express their complete childish dependence upon their will by pressing their foreheads to the earth. If life is not as happy for us as God means it to be for all children, we often try to find happiness when asleep by putting ourselves when in bed into the position we were in before birth. If we can get rid of the worries which are making us unhappy we sleep stretched out to our full length and what is called completely relaxed. When we can do this we wake from sleep refreshed and ready for the full life of a new day.

At birth we have to give up our old ways of getting food and air from the supplies which are carried by our mother's blood, and adopt instead mouth feeding; we also do our own digestion and expel the solid and liquid waste materials from the body through the anus and urethra. We have made all the organs ready for use and in a few hours we have to make this great change over. So our birthday is a very important occasion for us, at no other time in our lives do we experience so great changes in our way of living in such a short time.

When we have rested a few hours and had a good sleep we begin to look about for food, formerly the part of us in contact with our mother's womb has been our chief point of interest, but all that intricate apparatus has been detached from us, nothing but a little wound in the middle of our tummies remains and that soon heals over: the scar which we carry with us all our life we call the navel. Our chief point of interest now moves to our mouth and we soon begin to feel about with our lips to find the nipples through which we draw the milk which is to be our only nourishment for the next nine months or longer.

For many weeks our mouths are everything to us and they remain all our lives a point of interest and happiness: we eat, we kiss, we talk, we smile, we sing; for all these purposes we use our lips, but as you will soon realize we add to the mouth many other centres of interest and pleasure in the years during which we are growing up. Though the mouth is all-important to us the whole skin surface of our body is very sensitive. We find a spiritual contact with our mother through the skin; when we nestle up to her we get quite a lot of pleasure from the contact of her hands or those of others who love us and have the care of us. If the contact does not bring us happiness or if it is carried on when we really want to live a more independent life we may, when we are quite big children, resent being held, but the pleasure returns again when we are old enough to leave our parents' home and find a mate with whom we can start a new one.

While the mouth is our chief point of interest we use it to find and test everything. As soon as we have mastered the art of finding the way to the mouth with our hands we bring everything there. If we are frightened we use our mouths as do the animals. If you take a dog into a field of sheep and lambs you will see every lamb seek out its mother and pretend to draw some milk from her, this disposes of the feeling of danger. A shy child puts its fingers to its lips and many grown-up people cover up their mouths when a powerfully emotional person is talking. As suckling is a feminine act, that is, one of taking in, we need satisfaction in giving out from ourselves ♂; this we find in the elementary biting efforts of the gums and the pinching actions of the fingers. Some very self-assertive babies really hurt the mother and anyone else they are friendly with by the forcefulness of their pinching.

This letter must come to a finish. The child we are thinking about has ceased to be a tummy baby as my children used to call them, and is a pram baby. By the end of the next letter it will be almost out of the pram stage and be only needing the pushcart occasionally.

                      Your affectionate friend

VII

MY DEAR MARGARET,

In this letter I want to remind you about life in those early 3–4 years after the day you were born. Like everyone else you will not be aware of your memories of those years but they are there all the same. My first conscious memory was the birth of a younger brother when I was three years old. About half-past seven in the morning my sisters, whose room I shared, my elder brother from a room across the landing and the governess all ran down stairs. I got out of bed and followed them; after getting down two flights of stairs safely, I sat down in the middle of the third and cried until someone came out of my mother's room and carried me in to see the new arrival. I believe I turned away from him in disgust and dislike. Many years later earlier memories came to the surface and I could remember drumming my feet on the floor of my pram and being turned over and smackèd by my nurse for refusing to have my vest put on when being dressed one morning.

For a few months after birth we spend so much of our time asleep that our interests are almost exclusively in the mouth and the hands, but we slowly learn to focus our eyes and locate noises. I remember the delight of one baby who had for months listened to aeroplanes overhead when, lying in his pram, he was able to locate them with his eyes and follow them across the sky.

After a few months too we begin to show an interest in the evacuation of waste material from our bodies and this interest remains with us for several years. I remember my mother pointing out to me when I was a boy that when a baby was looking what was in those days called angelic, it was really occupied in the exercise of this normal functioning at the other end of its body. So fascinated are we by this achievement that babies will often learn to remove their napkins for the pleasure of handling their faeces. Later when we can walk the interest remains and it is quite normal for a child to want to keep the contents of its chamber to "show to Daddy" before it is disposed of. Sometimes our parents make much too much fuss about these things, or too much fuss of us, which has the same result, then faeces in symbolic form take an unduly large place in our emotional life as children and adults.

The interest may be transferred to dark-coloured food material. Sometimes the *form* this solid waste material takes, owing to the shape of our bowels, is a matter of transferred emotional interest. Many children find an inordinate attraction in sausages as a form of diet. Sometimes the interest remains in the form of a quite abnormal interest in dirt. Some people I have known are so much occupied with dirt that they work themselves to death trying to keep their houses spotlessly clean; they are people whose personality has been what we call fixated or anchored at this time of life. One friend of mine felt driven sometimes to exclaim to his wife: "For God's sake, my dear, let us have a bit of comfortable dirt"; his house was too spick and span for the use of ordinary folk.

It is all important to the development of men and women of the new age that substituted interests should not be forced upon us. I once met a nurse who had assisted at the arrival of over a thousand babies and claimed that she had never had a "dirty" one. Allowing for exaggeration, it is still appalling to think what a large amount of human unhappiness that woman had caused by imposing her will upon newborn infants. A wise mother serves and watches her children but does not impose her will upon them.

That the interest though suppressed is very widespread must be very obvious to you, if you ever glance at the cruder forms of picture post-card, especially those of German origin. Many jokes which highly intelligent people pass around are felt by them to be humorous solely because they stir up these early infantile interests.

The most frequent and the most serious transfer of faecal interest is to money or some form of personal property. It is this transferred interest which is responsible for the present breakdown of human co-operation in an age which we have deluded ourselves into believing highly civilized and Christian. Men have raised money to a place in the conduct of life where it has become the master, with the result that it has let loose the fiercest and most extensive display of destructive violence that history has ever known.

In this and the emotional stage of life I shall describe in my next letter, the colour black stands to us for strength. Many children are devoted to gollywogs or black dolls. So strong is the feeling that later in life many people think of black men as people physically much stronger than white, a belief which has no foundation in fact. The idea also probably accounts for the fact that it is in some parts of England considered lucky for a sweep to be the first person to wish good luck to a newly married couple.

The act of urinating is also a source of pleasure to a small child; a baby will often urinate upon the lap of someone of whom it is fond.

Though these natural functions are necessarily of very great importance to us in infancy we find many other satisfactions. It is an age when we especially appreciate regularity and habit and learn more by copying than by experiment. I have known a baby cry if the mother inadvertently replaced the powder pot on the mantelpiece at a spot where it was not customarily placed and to cheer up at once when the mistake was rectified.

Our objectivity often finds its satisfaction in noise; banging on a table with a spoon or later on a tin or a drum is a happiness of which the grown-ups are generally tired long before we have extracted all the gratification we want from the action. Then we soon acquire a choice in what we like to wear. A little girl, say of $2\frac{1}{2}$, will have very decided opinions as to her preference in dresses. Imitating mother in the handling of dolls and the attempting of the hundred and one domestic activities, sweeping, cooking, washing up, dusting, all help us to grow and develop our muscular powers until we are ready to move on into the age of emotional satisfaction. The practical way of learning has its drawbacks. I remember after I had used a poker to encourage a dining-room fire to greater cheerfulness, I missed the poker, only to discover that a daughter of two years of age was busily poking the red-hot bars of a gas fire in another room. There was of course nothing "naughty" in this action and it was not long before she learned what fires are poked and what are not. It would be well if the words "naughty" and "don't" could be removed from our nursery vocabulary. If we throw a broken tumbler into a dustbin and later find our baby has thrown her milk tumbler in too we were wrong in timing our action, not the baby who copied it.

Here is one more story to show how one little girl explained to her mother how she had moved from a mouth interest to the anal interest about which I have been telling you. She had for a long time described the actions of an imaginary sister who somewhere had a house and seven children. One day about the age of four she announced that the sister was dead, she had eaten so many potatoes she had burst. That sister was the child's female subjective self. The child was describing the end of her mouth phase of life, but that was not all; she went on to say that she had discovered another sister who had another little house. That other little house has its entrance at the other end of her body and for some years it will be the centre round which will be woven many happy phantasies. Happy the child whose mother and father can appreciate the fact that these phantasies are truth and who do not drive them into secrecy by calling them lies.

Your affectionate friend

VIII

MY DEAR MARGARET,

We have traced life up to the time when conscious memory begins for most of us. I have tried to show you the importance of sensations to us and how in addition we occupy our waking hours by copying the actions of all around us and developing our muscles so that we can function without effort. Our main interests still lie in eating and drinking and getting rid of the waste materials of digestion, of growth and muscular activity. The chief waste product of activity is a substance called urea; it is gathered up by the blood and sent out of the body through the kidneys, that is why we call the water discharged from the kidneys into the bladder urine. Slowly we add to an interest in the *sensations* of evacuation the *emotional* pleasures which accompany the actions.

In the emotional period of life the action of urine discharge means more to us than the sensation. I remember a little boy of four calling out to me across a garden to come and see how high he could project the stream of urine into the air. In the action he was demonstrating his objective masculinity, proving, very much to his own satisfaction, what a big man he was. When a small boy I had the company of a little girl about my own age for a year or more; she shared my nursery and my toys, we often shared the same big bath. I remember on one occasion we were punished by having dry bread (and tears) for tea because we were discovered competing as to the height we could project our urine up the garden wall. Much of the private conversation of small children centres on these functions and much harm is done by labelling them "dirty." As we come to a more advanced stage of development our interest drops away quite naturally and without any repression by grown-ups unless they themselves are fixated at this level of life and show it in their jokes and stories.

I explained to you in an early letter that everything in us has its dual form of expression; this is of course true of emotion. Fear ♀ and anger ♂, tears ♀ and laughter ♂ are opposites and it is a bad thing for us if we are made to shut down our tears or bottle up our anger in these years. Tears are a very healthy outlet for emotion and a great mistake is made when both boys and girls are urged to repress them as babyish.

One day a little boy about four years old showed me a chalk drawing of which he was very proud, a creative effort of his female self. I praised it and that somehow released his own pleasure in his work. This he expressed by destroying the picture with a pencil he had in his hand.

This is an example of the emotional satisfaction we get in hurting things. An early Stone Age man found the same satisfaction in the destruction of animals. Quite small children do not fear death or the taking of life and often show an interest in the killing of chickens or rabbits or other animals used for food. Under civilized conditions so many children are reared without any opportunity of coming up against the ordinary incidents of life on a farm that they turn to throwing stones at each other or hurting their neighbours' cats. Some get enough satisfaction in hitting the heads off flowers, or destroying their friends' toys. Often we wish to poison or otherwise remove those who thwart us.

The opposite of killing and hurting things and people is the enjoyment we get in being hurt ♀. Quite a lot of children, boys and girls, when they find other children or grown-ups too emotionally strong for them will fall down and cut their hands or their knees or cut themselves with a knife which at another time they could handle quite well without an accident. Tears are a much healthier reaction and when people have a little more understanding of life they will not be so contemptuous of tears. Subjective emotional excitement ♀ in many small children, boys as well as girls, affects their power of holding their urine. I have known many little girls who when they were thoroughly enjoying a game would wet their knickers and this is true too of boys whose personality is more subjective ♀ than objective ♂. It is probably true that the boys first have an emotional fear feeling and then get rid of this by wetting. They will often wet themselves if a teacher is angry with another child and not with them at all, girls will wet without any initial fear emotion.

To go on with our list of emotional pleasures, there is first the one of enquiry ♂, the desire to see how things work, especially do we want to know how animals and people produce offspring. A locked cupboard to a boy stirs up in him a desire to know what is inside, and both boys and girls with this inquisitive spirit get more pleasure from pulling a piece of clockwork to pieces and looking inside than in seeing it work. If we have not lived in a family where the bathroom door is always unlocked and Mummy and Daddy's bath is always an opportunity for conversation, if our questions about the new babies and the other practical things of life have not been answered fully, we are almost overcome by our thirst for knowledge; so much is this the case in some children that they are unable to give their attention to learning their letters and numbers and to mastering the art of reading. The opposite emotion ♀ is the desire to be looked at, to be loved with the eyes. In these days when healthy ideas about co-education are spreading many children are given full opportunity for getting happiness in this way. I was recently visiting a school where there were many happy boys and girls. When bed-time for the youngest group arrived, I went into one bathroom and talked to two girls in their baths and the boys washing at the basins; almost at once the matron came in to tell me the other bathroom occupants hoped I would soon go and visit them; of course I did, and found two boys in the baths and the girls cleaning their teeth and brushing their hair. When I was a youngster it was rare for parents and nurses to understand what a happiness it was to children to run about the house with nothing on. People had got so far from an understanding of God that they thought there was something indecent about the human body.

Though we have the new emotional ways of getting happiness we sometimes quickly go back to the old. I well remember as a small boy biting at the hands of those who I felt were interfering with my right of liberty. If you saw the film *David Copperfield*, you will remember the incident when David bites the hand of his stepfather. This is a return to mouth action owing to an unfortunate thwarting of the other male assertive activities I mentioned earlier in this letter. Sometimes also we go back to other infantile subjective reactions; we come out with sudden skin rashes, sore throats or swollen tonsils or we feel sick when there is nothing wrong with us to make us ill; we are really using our stomach to show that we dislike what some strong-minded person is saying to us or making us do.

At one time there was a wholesale removal of tonsils from thousands of children, now our doctors are getting more understanding of life and take the swollen tonsils as a sign that our environment is not a happy one and tell our parents to see what can be done about it.

> Your affectionate friend

IX

MY DEAR MARGARET,

There is still a lot to remind you about before we leave these nursery and kindergarten years of life. You will remember how acting games occupy very much of our time. Our imagination can make an aeroplane out of two sticks or a doll out of a rolled-up duster. We ourselves can be an engine pulling a long train or a nurse bandaging up wounded soldiers. One of the oldest games the world has known is played wherever children have the opportunity to get away from the overlooking eyes of grown-ups. Children, black, white and yellow, everywhere, play the doctor game. One child, not necessarily a girl, takes off some if not all of her clothes, unless like many black children she has none, then she is put to bed. The doctor comes and examines her, then another child is put to bed with her as the baby and he or she has to be fed. The game has many additions to it and by changing round the parts played, may be carried on for hours. It satisfies both the desire to see and the pleasure in being looked at and helps our bodies to grow healthily.

These years, too, are years when we appreciate music and dancing. All music was at one period of our history accompanied by movement and it is only the advanced civilizations which reach the stage when the people can sit still and listen to music.

The early music was an aid to dancing but the dancing came first. People danced when they ploughed their land, when they sowed the seed and when they harvested their crops. Some day you will enjoy a book by Naomi Mitchison, one of those people who can get out of time and bring the past into to-day. She describes in *Corn King and Spring Queen* the seasonal ceremonies, a mixture of dramatic performance and dancing, without which the people of earlier civilizations thought they could not secure good crops of corn and fruit.

In many European countries to-day dancing is still the chief form of emotional expression. They dance in spring and autumn, at births, weddings and deaths. In England the age of materialism has almost eliminated our old folk dances but in earlier times many villages had their own dances. Some were danced by teams of men in costumes, others were for the ordinary folk, both men and women. The English Folk Dance Society, founded by the late Cecil Sharpe, has managed to gather information about many of these dances and when the new age for which all the world is now struggling is born, we shall no doubt again give dancing the important place it should take in our lives.

To-day, to see dancing given its true place, you

would have to go to Bali, a Malayan island, Haiti, or some other of the islands off the coast of Central America, or to Africa. On the West Coast of Africa the people, where they have not been spoilt by our European customs of money-grabbing and our conceptions of decency and indecency, still dance on every occasion. They have both popular folk dances and the dramatic dances of professional men and women who are often part of the personnel of the tribal religious organization.

Have you ever tried to dance away your worries? If you haven't done so try it. Collect two or three records, *Anitra's Dance* or the *Dance of the Dwarfs* from *Peer Gynt* would do well, but the music need not be called dance music, then take off all the clothes you can so that nothing stops the air from circulating all round you. One piece of coloured material with a hole cut in for your head and something to pull it in at the waist makes a Greek costume. Set the record going, then let your legs and arms and later your whole body move about just as you feel the music tells you to. The clever writer of a book, *The Child's Path to Freedom*, Norman MacMunn, encouraged all the boys at his school to let themselves go in this way, and I have known both boys and girls enjoy themselves for hours dancing with no teacher but the music itself and their own wish to move in response to it.

Sometimes children are told that they are not

musical but music and measurement are part of the same thing, and it is certain that our bodies know all that there is to know about mathematics, the difficulty is to get that knowledge into our heads. The sort of free dancing I have described to you will at any rate give every boy and girl an opportunity to wake up their interest in music, and this helps them to understand all the arithmetical, geometrical and algebraical measurements with which our masters and mistresses have to fill our heads if we are to get a school-leaving certificate.

There is still one more emotional satisfaction I have not mentioned and that has as usual its two forms. One (♀) the subjective pleasure in making new music and the objective (♂) one of reproducing music on an instrument or in singing.

The animal ancestors of man all seem to have over-emphasized some particular characteristic all of which are found in man in a less complete form. Some biologists think this is why each animal family has remained unchanged for such a long time while the ancestors of man went on experimenting and changing until God led them into the time when he could bestow on them human consciousness. If we accept this interpretation of things then it is to birds that we have to look for the full emotional expression of themselves in sound. This is what Shelley meant when he wrote

LETTERS TO MARGARET

> "Hail to thee, blithe spirit!
> Bird thou never wert,
> That from heaven, or near it,
> Pourest thy full heart
> In profuse strains of unpremeditated art."

The skylark forgets itself in the ecstasy of emotion that it pours out hour after hour, filling the heavens with something more than sound. Birds also share with butterflies the pleasure in display of colour; this has no doubt a practical aspect of attraction to the mate for reproduction purposes, but that does not alter the fact that in these highly coloured birds the emotional pleasure in being looked at and looking takes precedence over other forms of satisfaction. During the emotional years we grow away from our mother, we are, or should be, weaned from complete dependence on her and experiment in emotional exchange with our fathers and other grown-ups round us and with other children. I remember at the age of about $4\frac{1}{2}$ being fascinated by a little girl of about three years who had been brought by her mother to afternoon tea at my home. During the whole visit I could not take my eyes off her, much to the amusement of the adults and my elder brothers and sisters. But such emotional friendships are quite temporary, before the end of these years we should be living a self-complete life. Psychologists use a long word for it which means we are in love with ourselves; they say we are narcissistic because of the Greek story of Narcissus who never grew up but remained a Peter Pan all his life. What it really means is that we are both boy and girl, ♂ and ♀, the parts of our bodies which we use for carrying on the race are still quite immature and are taking no part in shaping our lives. Unhappily it is true to say that very many children do not reach this happy state of life, part of them for one reason or another has become anchored in the earlier years, but with the increase of knowledge your generation will be able to give to its children opportunities for freedom to grow denied to so many in these years of blind struggle.

Your affectionate friend

X

MY DEAR MARGARET,

I expect you remember when you first started to lose your milk teeth and to grow what are called the permanent teeth. That time of transition marks a very important stage in human development. Until that time arrives we are what are called materialists or rationalists. The stories we like best are all about animals and we often use animals to portray for us the human beings who come and go around us without really being part of our world. Walt Disney has given us in Donald Duck and Clara Cluck and all the other animal people in his films a collection of characters which will give pleasure to several generations of children. But before the moving pictures, as they were first called, were invented animals acting as human beings formed the subject matter of children's books.

One of my favourite books as a small child was peopled with elephants and I can never forget the hare in *Struwel Peter* who commandeered the powder-horn and gun of the sleeping gamekeeper. Some years ago a big boy told me that he had a nightmare every night in which a big dog appeared to be sitting on the end of his bed. That dog expressed to him the male personality of his mother who had ordered and dominated every minute of his life since infancy.

With the change of teeth we enter a phase of life when imagination comes into play. Fairy stories and dreams replace the nightmares by which we formerly expressed as fear the libido dammed up within us.

Our fears of the dark, of the water from the lavatory cistern, of spiders or earwigs which as the dog in the boy's nightmare about which I have just told you stand for the male power in mothers, father, nurse, or the playful uncle who will toss us to the ceiling or carry us round the garden on his shoulder. All these fears slowly recede into the background, more easily so in a girl than in a boy, provided always that she is growing as nature intended her to grow,

In my last letter I told you that at the end of the emotional phase we are very complete little people neither male nor female, but with all sorts of bodily and emotional pleasures which express both parts of our personalities. Now new and interesting developments take place. In the first few years of adolescence, as it is called, we develop along the female side and that gives us a definite unbalance. We soon lose the feeling of self-completeness, just as at an earlier stage we lost the feeling of security resulting from dependence on our mothers. We now want to live less within ourselves and find happiness in a group life with others of our own age.

If we call 8–10 the years of transition, then 10–13 roughly correspond with the girl's puberty and the first half of adolescence. It has only been made clear in recent years that boys, though they do not possess the organs of reproduction of girls, have to travel through the girl's puberty and in doing so find some other outlet for the energy which in girls is being used to bring their bodies to maturity. You will remember my explaining to you how as new-born babies we use only the mouth as a means of satisfaction, that it was in fact the one place on the body where all interest centred, and how later the internal digestive apparatus and excretory apertures shared with the mouth as centres of attraction of libido. Now for the healthy girl there comes a new transference of interest. All the fears and the other ♀ emotional pleasures about which I have written to you, the father and mother games and such things also as identification of herself with her mother in the production of new babies, have all brought her to a point where the libido can be shifted to the organs of reproduction. The ovaries, the uterus or womb, the vagina which is the corridor leading to the womb and the entrance to the vagina, the vulva, have all been biding their time, but now they begin to bestir themselves. If the interest in black dolls and golliwogs has not gone by ten years it soon does, though an interest in dolls as symbols of the girl's own children-to-be may remain for some time.

Swinging on the branches of trees and similar experiences will often make the girl aware that changes are going on. Though most of the growth goes on behind the screen of the body wall, the chest area soon shows that the milk glands are growing in sympathy with the internal growth. Behind the nipples which are all the boy will ever have to show that he might have been a girl, the formerly flat level of the girl's chest almost imperceptibly rises as the breasts take form. Month by month growth proceeds, but especially at such times as the spring and early summer when new life and rapid growth is natural to all living things. Of course, we still have our emotional and physical pleasures: we want to run and play games, to shout and to cry, but imagination has its own language. For thousands of years men and women have been satisfied to learn by means of myths and fairy stories. Now is the time that we add to our equipment as human beings this new way of understanding. Every boy when he hears the story of Jack the Giant Killer or David and Goliath sees himself as the clever youngster who can conquer the father who all through his earlier years he has seen as an all-powerful giant; while every girl and boy sees in the mother, however loving she may be in reality, the all-powerful witch out of whose clutches he or she has to escape. I will have more to tell you about myths and fairy stories in later letters: there is enough in this one to occupy your thoughts for some time.

                        Your affectionate friend

XI

MY DEAR MARGARET,

In my last letter I described for you the changes which take place in the mental life of girls as they grow from the self-completeness at the end of the emotional years into the new life of the imagination, and reminded you of some of the bodily changes which occur at that time. To-day I will tell you something about the life of boys who also have to leave behind the stage of self-completeness but who have not female bodies to develop. My experience with boys and girls leaves me quite convinced that they can live far more happily and with far more consideration for one another if they are aware of the changes which are taking place in those of the other sex. Conscious knowledge not only helps to clear up their own difficulties but opens up for them a new companionship when the time comes for marriage. This has for a long time been the goal towards which human beings have been striving, but the lack of any real knowledge has increased the tension since women ceased to be what was called a chattel and obtained a political and social independence. A striving for mastery has wrecked many homes where a mutual understanding and co-operation would have brought peace.

LETTERS TO MARGARET

With the entry into the first half of adolescence, a boy begins to lose confidence in himself and this increases each successive year. As the girl's body develops, the boy, having the same instinctive desires, feels that there is something not quite right about his body. Many boys when in their baths or on some other occasion when they are without clothes, will push their sex organs out of sight between their legs, at the same time imagining themselves without them. Sometimes the libido which in the girl is being utilized in the rapid growth of her body but which in a boy is still present as anxiety may be directed to one part of the sex apparatus. He may be worried not that he has the male organs, but because of some imaginary fault in them. When this happens the worry may be unconsciously transferred to the eyes causing disturbed vision, which he later requires glasses to rectify.

As in the case of girls, boys should by now have left behind the interest in the waste material of the body and the digestive apparatus. This interest is projected outwardly and finds substituted satisfaction in hoarding or collecting other things. A boy may collect stamps, or cigarette cards, the numbers on engines, or motor cars, or he may collect apples or other fruit from orchards. At one time before they learned to cultivate the land our ancestors must have lived almost entirely by "collecting" honey from the wild bees, eggs from birds' nests, and every form of edible fruit or root which they found growing in the wild state. In the present age of private ownership when most things are the result of effort on someone's part, "collecting" becomes stealing.

In addition, while the girl is fitting herself for physical reproduction the boy sometimes finds compensation in making tunes to express his emotions and sometimes the instruments for making music. This is followed by other creative activities: modelling in clay, painting, and later the writing of poetry or the making up of imaginative stories. The boy's imagination also enables him to find satisfaction for his male self. When we are infants we have fantasies of being very powerful people, a cry will produce mother or food, and we think we have only to stretch out our hands with sufficient confidence to get hold of the moon. As the years of childhood go by we lose that means of satisfaction and adjust ourselves to reality as it is called. It now returns as imagination.

The creative activities I have mentioned give boys, and to a lesser extent and for a short time girls, satisfaction for the subjective ♀ desires, but the imagination also provides boys with a means of compensating themselves for the loss of confidence inevitable on their entry into adolescence. Some years ago a boy at my school who was very much attached to his mother spent almost a whole term making an island of plasticine, giving it trees, buildings, animals, etc., and also a set of telephone poles and wires. One day I found that he had made a plasticine cart and had piled all the farm equipment and telephone poles on it. On enquiry I found that the man who owned the island had decided to move on. The boy's imagination had created a world from which he could keep in touch with his mother. The islander's decision to leave the island was the boy's decision to find his own feet. On a subsequent holiday I had a letter from his mother asking if he could return to school before the end of the holidays as he was tired of London.

Though the old fairy stories are not now given the attention they had before the time of cheap printing, there is plenty of imaginative writing about. You know all about the current volumes which deal with adventures at school and every week the old fairy stories appear in some new guise in the weekly boys' papers, and the girls' too. Stories of the clever boy overcoming the wicked uncle or other villain, and the girl who outwits the wily schemings of the hated stepmother.

Imagination then in its subjective ♀ form and objective ♂ form marks the next great stage in the development of the human race. Primitive man used it in making his picture languages the form in which he first wrote his thoughts. We use it in ways not understood to encourage ourselves to become more civilized. We identify ourselves with our heroes, use them to express something in us we feel to be worth while, and in so doing our imaginations help us to grow like them. A boy will thus develop the fighting and hunting instincts and the girl the maternal which she sees expressed by the arrival of her younger brothers and sisters or the children of the other households which form the social community of which her home is a unit.

To our imagination we owe also all the inventive genius which has provided man with a substitute for manual labour. As the first man to send a picture message to a fellow hunter is re-lived in every boy who invents a secret language, so the men who found safety by building houses in the trees for the better protection of their families live again in the imagination of every boy who has access to the country.

He looks up and sees some branches which are nearly on a level. Up comes the idea of a house in a tree. Then follows ideas about ropes to haul up what he wants, about how to get up and down easily, notching the trunk or making a rope-ladder. In this way his imagination brings to the surface ancestral memories. He has been taught from inside (intuition). In the same way at another time the ancestral memory working through the imagination urges him to dig out a cave to live in, or make a boat out of withies, string and canvas or anything else he can lay his hands on.

God in leading the human race from the instinctive life of animals into a state of conscious understanding provided in the imagination a means of linking the seen with the unseen and of bringing into the present the manifold experiences of the thousands of years that have measured man's progress.

Your affectionate friend

XII

MY DEAR MARGARET,

It is now a full year since I started for you this series of letters. You are now in your thirteenth year and each month sees you growing happily in the direction of full physical functioning. This point in time may soon be reached and you will then be capable of carrying on the race. In another letter I will tell you why the greater part of the human race has postponed the actual use of the body for the production of offspring for several years after the time when pregnancy, as it is called, is possible. Female animals in the wild state function in this way as soon as the ovaries have commenced to produce the egg cells. You will later come to realize that we are human because we have learned to use our reproductive energies for other purposes than procreation, a word which means the production of children. This postponement does not in any way reduce the satisfaction which is felt by a girl when she knows she has passed the new mile-stone on the road to adult life.

Your biology book will have told you how within the ovary certain cells are set apart for reproduction and how at the right time one or more of these cells ripen, throw off part of the nuclear material and then burst through the wall of the ovary and travel down the ovarian duct. This is not all that happens; at the same time as the egg is ripening the ovary secretes a hormone, a sort of messenger carried by the blood which tells the cells forming the wall of the uterus to prepare for the attachment of the egg and the subsequent feeding of the embryo. Generally in human beings one egg is formed each month, but this can only anchor itself if it has been joined by a male sperm. The uterus prepares itself for a fertilized egg, but should the egg fail to anchor itself, the lining cells of the uterus and the tiny blood vessels that feed them break down and form what is called in medical terminology the menstrual period. Some females are so sensitive that they are aware of tension in the right or left ovary whichever contains the fully formed egg cell, but otherwise the whole process should be entirely free from pain and is usually so if it is commenced during the early years of adolescence. When visiting a school some years ago, I well remember the first individual I met as I turned from the road up the drive-way was a girl of thirteen who dashed out of the shrubbery to tell me her period had started. She was as pleased and happy as later she will be when she knows she is "in child," as it is called, or as a father when he sees his first son or daughter. Sometimes for a few months there is irregularity of functioning, but in far the greater number of females the first period is followed by another in twenty-eight days and subsequently every twenty-eight days for the subsequent thirty to forty years, except during the time when the uterus contains a growing child and for the few months after its birth. As twenty-eight days is also the moon's cycle the moon before the age of science was thought to have a close association with women and to influence their lives. At first the moon was thought to be male and was considered the actual father of all children. In the German language it is still male. From this position it came to be the special property of women and then to be a woman and we now talk of the moon as "she" and the sun, symbol of the male fertilizing partner of the woman, as "he."

The first stage of adolescence through which you are passing and which finishes shortly after the first menstrual corresponds, as I told you in my last letter, with the development of imaginative mental activity. In dreams the inner physical growth is often portrayed in pictorial form. Dreams of water, of being reborn, or of incidents in which red objects or blood itself plays a part are very common, as are dreams of secret caves and treasure houses or treasure chests filled with jewels of unbelievable beauty. We each of us develop our own dream language and it is helpful if at an early date we learn to translate it into conscious word form. In those periods of man's history before conscious intellectual understanding had been de-

LETTERS TO MARGARET

veloped or was in abeyance, the imagination was the most mature channel of understanding and expression. Over a long period of history of the people of Egypt, for example, there was a half human, half animal god symbolic of every character which goes to make up a human being. I expect you remember visiting the British Museum and seeing the hawk-faced, lion-faced and numerous other gods. The imagination delights in symbolism and understands it; by the word "understand" I do not mean consciously interprets it, but is unconsciously aware of what the picture language is saying. When we are grown up we still use the imagination and every conversation is full of symbolic meaning which does not require to be translated in order to be understood. I shall have more to tell you about the imagination later as symbolism is the language which does most to enrich religions and serves largely to convey to us their hidden truths.

I want now to translate for you one fairy story which expresses in symbolic language the stage in the life of a girl which I have been describing for you in this letter. You will remember how in the story of Sleeping Beauty the girl in the absence of her parents goes up a forbidden tower, finds a loom left by an old woman who works there, pricks her finger and goes to sleep for a hundred years until the Prince finds her and wakens her with a kiss to be his bride. Here is the story translated into intellectual from imaginative language. The forbidden tower is the vagina, the passage way into the uterus which in the first eight or nine years plays little or no part in a girl's life but which in early adolescence makes rapid growth in size and sensitiveness. The weaving loom at the top of the tower, the existence of which has been unknown until the tower has been explored, is the uterus. Here at the top of the tower mother nature (the old woman) incessantly plays her part in creating each successive generation. The pricked finger is the menstrual flow and the hundred years of sleep are the subsequent years of adolescence until maturity.

Often fairy stories are frightening to children if given to them in early childhood when everything is "real" and the imagination dormant, but at your age you should enjoy the wonderful sagas of the heroes of Asgard and the myths of all nations now available in English. Let your imagination drink deeply of these old stories handed down from mouth to mouth for hundreds of years before they were either written or printed. If you do you will find later that you possess the imaginative key which admits you into comradeship with the poets.

Your affectionate friend

XIII

MY DEAR MARGARET,

The entry into the final stage of physical growth, which for the girl is marked by the commencement of the menstrual flow, has always been an important occasion, as is the entry into full male functioning to a boy. Many tribes inhabiting the Pacific islands and in Africa mark the event by ceremonials, which have as their object the purpose of aiding girls to play their parts adequately and happily as women. European races have suffered by dropping such ceremonies and substituting a symbolism which should have enriched the ceremony and not replaced the physical instruction.

In the walls of the vagina there are fibres of connective tissue which sometimes pass across the passage way itself; they are the embryonic remains of fibres which in a boy obliterate the female reproductive organs. These fibres are called the Hymen; they are often broken during the doctor games of childhood or by the exploring finger of a girl herself during early adolescence. The initiation ceremonies have as their main purpose the dilation of the vaginal passage and the breaking of any remaining fibres. In one period of Greek history this was one of the duties of the priests in the temples as it was the responsibility of the

Jewish priests to circumcise a boy child at birth. In some African tribes it is also the work of the priests to perform the initiation ceremony of girls, in others it is the responsibility of elder women; in other tribes it is left to the girls themselves. The Bantu girls, when they have reached puberty, pass small pullets' eggs into and out of the vagina, later they use eggs of larger size, until the time comes when they can pass in and out without breaking it a full-sized hen's egg. They then go to their mothers and tell them that they are ready for marriage. You will remember my telling you that during the years of the girl's puberty boys often transfer the worries about the unsuitability of their sex organs to the eyes and in so doing distort their vision. In the same way a girl tends to transfer the tension in an undilated vagina to her eyes, nose, or throat. Nature intends all organs to be very much alive and the sexual apparatus of a girl when capable of functioning should react to all her subjective emotions, secreting from its surface and the Cowper glands a glutinous substance which is a lubricant. An unhealthy vagina like a paralysed hand denies the owner part of the normal means of self-expression. In place of the natural lubricant in a non-active vagina an opaque semi-solid substance accumulates; for this reason many mothers of to-day take their daughters to a doctor with the request that the vagina be given the required dilatation. Some African tribes extend the ceremony by adding what amounts to an operation. At the upper end of the vulva beneath the skin there is, as you know, a small body which is called the clitoris; it is the bud which would have grown into a penis if the girl had become a boy. In the early years before the female sex organs have sprung to life this organ is capable of giving pleasurable sensations, and many girls discover some way of stimulating it to activity as does the boy his penis even within the first year of life. Now the erection of the clitoris is a male objective satisfaction, so some tribes include the removal of it as part of the initiation ceremony for girls. The acceptance of pain is part of life and during this operation the girl is expected to remain quite still and free from emotion, otherwise she is considered to have let down her sex. This way of putting the clitoris out of action is not a necessity in order to rid a girl of objective satisfaction because as the vagina and uterus develop the libido finds in them new centres of attraction. Most girls who have used the clitoris as an outlet for emotion in childhood feel at about the age of fourteen that there is something wrong in doing so, which means that they feel that the sensations experienced are not consistent with the proper functioning of their sexual apparatus. They then break themselves of the habit and soon experience in dreams the more mature and equally pleasurable reactions of the vagina and uterus.

LETTERS TO MARGARET

In the Christian Church there is as I have reminded you a pubertal ceremony which ignores the body and has really a closer relation to the ceremonies of entry into adult life at the end of adolescence but it is often gone through even before the female functioning has commenced. This ceremony of Confirmation, as it is called, has two objects, one is the admittance of an adolescent into full membership of the Church with responsibility for his or her own actions which he or she then takes over from the God-parents. Secondly, and of much more religious importance, the surrender of the individual boy or girl to God or the unseen power from which each individual life is separated or partly separated, and if human is able to become aware of its individuality. The symbolism of the communion service makes use of the mouth satisfaction of infancy. The bread and wine taken into the body via the mouth symbolize the spiritual inflow ♀ and helps to balance the objective life which comes into prominence during the boy's pubertal years, the second stage of adolescence.

I want you to read carefully the Io myth which you will find in *The Age of Fable* and most other volumes of tales of Greek mythology. This story describes in the language of the imagination the life of any normal girl from the end of childhood to the end of adolescence. I have given the story in full in my book *Psychological Foundations*. At the commencement of the story Io is a very lovable person but not of course ready for the adult forms of the expression of love. In order to protect her the goddess Juno turns her into a heifer. Io then loses her old ways of expressing her feelings, she is in a state of transition and has to content herself with scraping on the ground with her hoofs the information that she is herself. Argus of the thousand eyes in whose charge she is placed is conscience which holds in it the experiences of the past ages. Conscience, very active at the beginning of the story, is eventually put to sleep by Mercury. That which is at first feared in course of time becomes something beautiful. As in the "Beauty and the Beast" story the dreaded Beast becomes the Prince, here the eyes of conscience become the "eyes" in a Peacock's tail. Io is not yet ready for adult life. The gadfly bites her and she experiences the difficult period between adolescence and adult life, generally a girl's eighteenth or nineteenth year. After traversing this period safely, Io regains her human form and with it finds her capacity for a full human love relationship.

Your affectionate friend

XIV

MY DEAR MARGARET,

In this letter I am proposing to fill in the picture by describing the period from eleven to thirteen in boys. The struggle between the urge to physical and emotional female expression of the libido and the development of mental creative powers, which I described in an earlier letter, continues through these years. Some boys will even have monthly nose bleeding or monthly attacks of indigestion but they are boys with an early love fixation. The boys without such anchorings will find expression for the urge to create in some form of craftsmanship —hut making, tool making, the making of weapons for hunting—later they will express their anxiety by painting or creative writing.

Primitive civilizations have sometimes tried to eradicate the female element in man altogether before the entry of the boy into adult life. Experience taught men the truth that when we overdo the expression of one side of life we tend to swing over to its opposite. Advantage was taken of this to try to concentrate as much fear and pain into a few months of a boy's life in the hope that it would produce the opposite and make him as a man an efficient warrior.

LETTERS TO MARGARET

The transition period from the end of the girl's puberty into the male puberty was used for a prolonged period of training which finished with the initiation ceremonies into manhood. Boys were starved, beaten, kept in the dark, had their teeth and hair pulled out, frightened by instruments called bull roarers and by masked figures arriving by boat at the island and supposed to represent the gods. The boys with a weak physical constitution or a strong balance towards subjectivity often died under the ordeal. If they lived but were considered failures by the tribal chiefs whose one idea was to produce fighters, they were returned to the care of their mothers and were often later poisoned.

Some communities which, viewed by European standards, appear uncivilized had far more knowledge of the two-sided character of the human personality. These tribes allotted some of the more subjective boys to the priesthood or agriculture and the objective to the hunter and warrior class.

When a boy reaches the time when, if a girl, he would have started his menstrual period he should have found a new confidence through his creative ability, but the physical inadequacy is still an important factor in his life and this often makes him appear shy in comparison with a girl of the same age. It is now that the male side of the personality comes to the fore. Under the guidance of the hormones from the pituitary gland, a tiny gland at the base of the brain which has so much to do with our growth, both boys and girls develop the objective (♂) personality and are enriched by the expansion of the male intuition and the power of abstract reasoning. For the boy there is also increase in the activity of the testes which, sending hormones into the blood, cause the growth of hair on the pubic surface of the body as did the ovarian internal secretion for the girl and also in the boy the growth of hair on the face. Changes also slowly take place in the sound apparatus at the top of the wind-pipe. The boy's voice first "breaks," as it is called, and then re-forms at a lower note varying from a deep base to a tenor. Right from infancy boys take pleasure in the erection of their combined urinating and sex organ, the penis, but without any glandular discharge. Sometimes, however, owing to the overstimulation of dominating adult personalities or the cultivation of habits learned from older but unenlightened boys, the prostate gland—a gland which lies near the base of the penis where it connects with the bladder—may be induced to function during the time of the girl's puberty. If this happens then or in the early part of the male puberty the use of the penis may be linked with anxiety. As the organ is essentially male and assertive in its action this linking with the female side of the personality spells unhappiness. Left alone the prostate gland and the testes come to

LETTERS TO MARGARET

function two or three years later when the positive assertive personality is uppermost. I will tell you more about that in a later letter.

Owing largely to a faulty environment in infancy but partly to heredity some girls do not follow the natural course of development I have described to you as normal. You must know many girls older than yourself among your school friends who are almost as flat-chested as they were at nine years old. Many do not start their menstrual period until fifteen or sixteen years of age. Just as the premature functioning of a boy's glands lead him to associate their activity with the presence of anxiety, so the delayed functioning in the girl results in the linking of the activity of her sex organs with her objective male personality. This means a constantly repeated struggle between the subjective and objective life, which is shown in two or three days' excitement each month and then physical pain before the menstrual flow commences.

To right this inverted attachment necessitates a period of re-education before or after marriage, if there is to be full acceptance and delight in the man or woman's part in coitus. I have often reminded you that boys and girls carry in their memories all the experiences of the opposite sex and gave you as an example that girls to some extent share with boys the pleasure in creative artistry and the expression by this means of their subjective life. This in the early years of the boys' puberty, though continuing for them, dies down for girls. The technique which has been acquired is not of course lost and can be developed, but the work becomes less and less an expression of the inner life and more and more objective. By that I mean that a girl will put into her drawings more of what she sees and less of herself. For the same reason that a girl, before she approaches maturity of body, shares a boy's creative (♀) interests, so also in this early stage of male puberty she shares his hunting interests. Every girl, though to a variable extent, is an Atalanta and in competitive games, sports and genuine hunting activities can be a comrade to a boy without losing any of that active physical growth which fits her for eventual motherhood.

       Your affectionate friend

XV

MY DEAR MARGARET,

The thought may have come to you that now, if from the point of view of functioning a girl is a woman at thirteen years of age, it is strange that there are so many years to go by before marriage. The answer to that question lies in the fact that the higher levels of mental life have been reached by mankind owing to the postponement of the time of full physical functioning and the use of the libido for mental or spiritual growth.

The story of man's exit from the Garden of Eden expresses imaginatively the step on the road from instinctive to conscious life. At one time girls were married at puberty and were old women at thirty, and this practice has been reverted to in India where the date of marriage is still very early, so much so that girls have often not given up their dolls before they have their first baby. This early functioning shuts the girls off from further individual development and leaves them childishly dependent on their husbands. So much so that it was at one time the custom for a widow to destroy herself on the funeral pyre which was burning up her late husband's remains. With man's step to consciousness, symbolized by the eating of the tree of knowledge, men and women were no longer controlled solely by their instincts as are all animals below the level of man. This period of history or rather pre-history corresponds with the adolescent years thirteen to maturity. Man became during that period of his evolution a conscious and religious animal. "Adam and Eve," that is to say the men and women who were our ancestors at this stage of human evolution, were driven out of the "Garden of Eden" where instinct alone ruled and struggled along the road of understanding until they could consider themselves true sons of God and co-operate with him for their further development. The postponement of marriage, that is of the function of reproduction, on the part of girls is also of the utmost importance to the male half of the race. Let me remind you again of our joint mental heritage, then you will see how every step forward women make affects the boys of the future, and *vice versa* the advances of men affect the girls of the future. The late J. D. Unwin by his research described in his book *Sex and Society* has demonstrated very conclusively that if girls delay maternity until the end of adolescence, the mental life of the young men is enriched and they both use a higher form of religion than do those of races where early physical association is common. The postponement of marriage in India to the end of adolescence would most certainly reduce the number of men who feel impelled to seek happiness on a physical basis, in masochism or self-torture, crawling for hundreds of miles on their hands and knees, sleeping on beds and nails, etc. Their appreciation of religious truths would be found less in physical ways, and more by means of the emotion of the imagination. A second important discovery which J. D. Unwin explains in his last book, *Hopousia*, is that a custom can be fixed in the memory of a people after three generations, after which it is followed intuitively in a suitable environment. If the people of India decided to postpone the marriage of their girls to, say, the age of nineteen and of their young men to twenty-one years and were able by propaganda and religious appeal to carry that out through three generations the custom would then, it may be assumed, be fixed in the unconscious mind and the instinctive urge to early marriage would be overruled by the intuitive desire to postpone it until maturity as is the custom in Europe. It would be conscience (intuition) *v.* instinct, with the likelihood of conscience winning in a large proportion of people. This protective conscience, the "Argus" of the Io story, enables boys and girls in Europe to work and live happily together through adolescence without being driven by instinct to satisfy the urge to reproduction.

You can be quite certain that those girls and boys

who are always talking about the sexual life of adults, often with the idea that they are saying something very grand and very naughty, are in reality some of the numerous unfortunates who as children have been denied both the knowledge and the experiences which belong to childhood. The boy or girl who has had all his or her questions answered stage by stage, and has lived in a free boy and girl environment of a family or a co-educational school, is not in these adolescent years interested in sex life as a topic of conversation. The girl at this time, confident in her normality, and a few years later the boy also, feels and rightly feels the greatness of the spiritual power which has come to them and they prefer to express their innate interest in the form of poetic and religious symbolism. Eventually, of course, at the end of adolescence this spiritual power will find its expression in mature physical companionship. In the meantime as adolescents we get all we require in the way of libido exchange in the form of what has been called friendship-love. Much that I have to tell you about the objective imagination must be left for another letter, but I must just refer to the fact that it is by means of the objective ($\male$) and subjective ($\female$) intuition that true friendship establishes itself. The flow of libido in this unconscious way can be from boy to girl, from girl to girl, or from boy to boy. The only essential is that one plays the objective male role, and is in fact the giver and lover, and the other the receptive role and is the loved, the receiver and often the server.

We may have many such friendships during the adolescent years, the role played in one friendship may be reversed in the next. In this way we slowly fit ourselves for the more mature friendships of later life when there is to and fro flow or alternating objective and subjective attitude of mind. Friendship-love should mean greater pleasure in life and better school work, and the establishment of such love relationships is one of the soundest arguments for co-educational schools. Do not be afraid to love your friends but choose as friends either boys or girls of about your own age. The teachers who have a passionate friendship with his or her pupils or those who stimulate pupils to a passionate adoration of himself or herself are examples of people with inhibited and anchored personalities.

Your affectionate friend,

XVI

MY DEAR MARGARET,

In the course of these letters I have tried to show you how step by step the human personality has been enriched in the course of evolution and how each new life, boy or girl, has to re-climb the ladder. We started with sensation in its dual form then added to them the dual form of emotion. Then when thinking about the early years of adolescence we added the subjective intuition with its power of creative imagination. Now we are looking forward into the years of male puberty we can think about the objective imagination which is also intuitive and the objective intellect. That will leave one more mental function, the subjective intellect, to add to our list; you will then be able to think of a human being as eight-sided. Do you remember my early letter about the sixth sense? If not it would be well to look it through again, as it will help you to understand God's wonderful gift to man, the objective intuition. Neither you nor I can understand how the unconscious mind of one person can contact and bring to the surface what is in the mind of someone else and recount for them with astounding accuracy past experiences, or, stranger still, tell them, if not what will happen to them, what at any rate under the existing circumstances is likely to be the course of events in the coming years of their life; we only know that these things cannot be denied by anyone with a reasonably open mind. People with this specially developed power are the clairvoyants and dowsers. They have been recognized as exceptionally gifted in every age, sometimes looked up to and valued, sometimes feared. In the middle ages of our European civilization many thousands of women with this mental power very much in evidence were burnt at the stake as witches. The priests of the famous Delphic Oracle made use of women gifted in this way to answer the questions of those who came for guidance. From the ground in the neighbourhood of the temple there issued a gas which had an asphyxiating effect. The women used for the purpose of foreseeing events were stupefied by this gas and then had the questions put to them. Certain races have this mental attribute more developed than others; the gypsies have told fortunes wherever they have wandered about Europe. There are, however, far more people with this gift than are recognized or are prepared to acknowledge it to themselves. Too much education of the conscious intellectual kind tends to obliterate it. The Arabs have used boys as diviners, and the writer of a sixteenth-century manuscript says, when advising as to the procedure to be adopted, "the child either a maid or a boy should not be more than twelve years old." Though the function is intuitive and cannot be consciously influenced it is generally exercised by means of a material instrument. A dowser seeking for hidden springs of water holds a hazel twig in his hand. This will be twisted or sometimes broken by unconscious muscular movements, induced by his intuitive mental activity when he locates an underground stream or reservoir. Many men who have acknowledged and developed this power use a small weight on the end of a string which moves under the influence of the unconscious activity of their minds. Mirrors of polished metal, glass or crystal balls, and the water in shallow wells, have all been used as objects on which attention can be concentrated in order to enable the clairvoyant to function intuitively.

You will no doubt, in time, hear a lot about automatic writing, table turning and many other things which have been attributed to the influence of spirits. All I want to say to you about such happenings is that wise people do not jump to conclusions. We are slowly learning about the human mind and its powers and it is by no means necessary to accept as explanations of things we do not understand the continued influence of those who have died. If in the next year or two you get to know the writings of the great mystics, Chinese, Indian and Hebrew, you will have

LETTERS TO MARGARET

so adequate an inner consciousness of the non-material world that you will never feel the urge to gain evidence by such material means as appeal to those who attend spiritualistic séances. Make a start with the Book of Psalms in the edition of the Hebrew and Christian books called "The Bible intended to be read as Literature."

The question of getting back out of present time into the past is another power which is possible only through the male objective intuition. Many people are sensitive to incidents which have taken place in buildings during occupation by former tenants. They will say, "I like the feel of this house, happy people have been here or in this room," or on the other hand, "I feel there has been some unhappiness here and could never live here in comfort." Many so-called haunted houses must be places where strongly emotional incidents have taken place and intuitive people feel that those incidents are always being re-enacted.

What is likely to become a classical example of this power is the experience of Ann E. Moberly and Eleanor F. Jourdain when in the grounds of the palace of Versailles in 1911; they are given in their book, *An Adventure*.*

Some people have one psychological attribute strongly developed, others another. It would be no

* Published with a preface by Edith Oliver and a note by J. W. Dunne. Faber and Faber, Ltd. (London).

good a man attempting to be a pugilist who had not at his disposal objective physical force, nor would it be any use a man or woman attempting to sing in opera without a big reserve of emotional force; but that does not mean that we ordinary folk cannot take up boxing or sing for our own pleasure if we want to. I have purposely focused your attention upon those people who have an over-emphasis of the objective intuition so as to make clear to you how the objective imaginative level of the mind enriches our lives. This quality of mind is available for all and is used far more than most people are aware. It can give us the capacity for sympathetic understanding of the troubles of a friend without the necessity of a great deal of explanation. It enables some people to know just who to put to do this or that piece of work instead of trying to fit a square peg into a round hole. By its use many magistrates are able to cancel out the false evidence which has been freely poured out intentionally and unintentionally at the hearing of a court case, and give a fair judgment upon the issue. It enables one person's balance of mind and depth of experience to be made available to others and so share round their greater wealth of understanding. Best of all perhaps it links up those who have a common perception of religious truth, enabling them to lose the feeling of isolation and to help them to a realization of God's purpose for them and for the world. In the next few years you will be making great use of the objective intellect; about which I shall have something to tell you in my next letter. When as adolescents we add it to our other means of perception school work becomes much easier. You will have to use it to a considerable extent if you decide on a university course. Practise as well a physical and mental relaxation in your approach to poetry, drama, and the work of the great masters in music and the arts. If you do so you will be using your objective intuition to enable you to appreciate their subjective experiences and gain an understanding of their minds which no intellectual study of their work can ever give you.

       Your affectionate friend

XVII

MY DEAR MARGARET,

After my first few letters to you I began to tell you about the stages of life from birth and have since that date described to you incidents in the life of children younger than yourself. The descriptions were intended to help you to revive and re-live your early years and to put those incidents in their right relationship to your life of to-day. Now your position in time is changed whatever I say in the remaining letters, so far as it is true, will be already known to you, that is, to the inner world of your unconscious mind, but it will be about things you have not yet experienced. Instead of looking back you will be looking forward. Whenever we gain a new faculty we want to try it out on our old knowledge and this is especially evident when we develop the objective intellect. When you come to realize that you are understanding things in a new way, you will, for example, find a new interest in these letters and will do well to re-read them. Many of the things the educational system tries to teach us in early years would be far better left out of our school curriculum until this way of understanding is available to us. We can of course accumulate many facts by the use of the memory, but if as children we were allowed to understand with our emotion and intuition until fifteen or sixteen years old we would then have the intellectual function as a new delight and could fit ourselves for passing the university matriculation or get the school-leaving certificate by a few months of hard work.

The objective intellect follows hard on the objective intuition, but the increase of objective power which comes with the boy's puberty shows itself also in an increase of the emotional life of girls and their capacity for physical activity in games and work. This is all to the good and adds to the zest of living, provided always that there is no attempt to rob the subjective life of libido to feed the objective. A boy's physical and emotional power is not now as high as a girl's. He is growing rapidly and the sex glands are approaching maturity. Somewhere round his sixteenth birthday the prostate gland and the testes themselves start to function. Many boys, after a restless week or two, wake from a vivid dream to find that semen, which has the consistency of white of egg, has been ejected from the penis. This should be a proud moment in the life of every boy and give him a confidence in his well-being corresponding to that of the girl when she has her first menstruation. Unfortunately, for many boys the event does not have this result. In the depths of the unconscious minds of many lurks the memory of the displeasure shown to him by an impatient nurse or overworked mother before he had grown out of the habit of wetting his bed. The use of his penis as a channel of exit for seed revives these memories and many boys, denied the help and understanding of the father, which should be his right, feel instead of satisfaction only anxiety. So common is this reaction that the word pollution has been used extensively for this discharge which is as pure, and free from anything dirty, as is the milk which flows to us from our mothers' breasts.

At first, perhaps once a month and later fortnightly or even weekly, this flow of semen takes place as the glands, even in a semi-dormant state of the late adolescent years, form both internal and external secretions. The internal secretion is added to the blood stream and supplements the male hormone of the pituitary gland present also in girls. The quantity of the internal secretion varies considerably, with the result that some boys live a more subjective life than others and tend to be more passive (♀) in their friendship-love relationships, a girl or another boy playing the part of the emotional giver (♂). The variation does not affect their ultimate power of procreation, and for both types the libido through the final years of adolescence is available for use in their mental life, if they do not attempt to precipitate matters by self stimulation and so reach full functional activity of the glands some time before the date for the normal maturity for their race.

In those races where the full output of libido is required for hunting and fighting a boy is initiated into the technique of active sex life soon after his glands have commenced to function. He is given instruction how to link his sexual apparatus with that of a female, in what is called coitus. But such early activity cuts the man off from further mental development as does too early maternity the mental growth of women.

During the final pubertal years of boys, girls have a somewhat similar surrender to make as the un-anchored boys made during the girls' puberty. They often dream of losing a hand, their tongue or a foot, all of which express in symbol their surrender of the right to the male organs of reproduction. This sacrifice is all the easier if the girl's puberty has been fully and adequately achieved in the ways I have described to you. Also if there is adequate scope for the expression of their objective lives through the functional channels of the emotion and intuition.

Both boys and girls in the final adolescent years can appreciate the ceremonial and objective symbolism of religious services, and whenever an attempt is made to do without such intuitive aids to understanding the whole level of life is reduced. Rationalism and materialism, the reduction of all life to a level from which the emotional and intuitional channels of perception are cut out, make of men and women something far less than human and allows them to do things from which animals are barred by their natural instincts.

In addition to the objective intuition and intellect the boy, if he has used his subjective intuition in creative artistry, has added to his powers that of subjective intellectual functioning. This tendency to subjective mental activity on the part of boys appears to give many girls an unfair advantage in competitive examinations as they can with greater ease concentrate on objective thought and memorization. The fact is that after the pre-pubertal balanced years, the male and female travel very different roads. I shall have something to tell you about those roads later. Though the routes are very different the totality of experience over a wide stretch of years should bring men and women to a point where they can travel a common path again in the years beyond middle life.

Your affectionate friend

XVIII

MY DEAR MARGARET,

The boy and girl whose lives we have been following are now approximately sixteen years old, but there is still some little distance to travel before the end of adolescence. Under the British law both men and women are responsible for themselves from the age of twenty-one, but the women of Northern Europe are generally as mature at nineteen as the man at twenty-one or even older. They may not, however, enter into marriage without the consent of their parents or a magistrate until they are legally of age.

There must be few either of men or women who have not experienced in their late adolescent years the emotional experience of falling in love, so that must be the main subject of this letter. The basis of falling in love lies in the powers of identification and projection. We see in the object of our love characteristics which complete our own personality and project upon them part of our own emotional selves. If both people are in love at the same time there is both a loss and an enrichment. If the man has an objective personality he sees in the woman the essence of femininity, she sees in him the ideal objective male. Sometimes it is the other way round, the man sees in the woman strength and security and she in him a creative ability which she is drawn to stimulate into activity. Whichever way the projection works the two are for the time being one. Here is the idea expressed in verse by Sir Philip Sidney:

> "My true love hath my heart, and I have his
> By just exchange one for another given:
> I hold his dear, and mine he cannot miss,
> There never was a better bargain driven:
> My true love has my heart, and I have his.
>
> His heart in me keeps him and me in one,
> My heart in him his thoughts and senses guides:
> He loves my heart for once it was his own,
> I cherish his because in me it bides:
> My true love has my heart, and I have his."

Sometimes this feeling of being in love is a one-sided affair. I can remember at the age of sixteen cycling between three and four miles and parading the streets in the neighbourhood of the house of a girl I had met when on holiday. If after an hour or so chance gave me an oppotrunity of taking off my hat to her, I felt well rewarded and returned home to settle down to my school prep. or to join the rest of the family in a game of table tennis. Often behind such temporary attractions lies the memory of a love association from the earlier years of life. Do you remember my telling you that with each new phase of our development we want to revive old associations and express them in terms of our new functional activity? This desire is very strong when we reach physical maturity and many of the brief love affairs in late adolescence are revivals of reactions dating right back to infancy. A "Don Juan" is a man who never gives up hunting for a substitute for the mother image which he carries in his mind, but all of us are attracted by the ears, the eyes, the hair and other physical characteristics of people we meet because we can thereby identify them with those people we have formerly loved or have loved us. These partial love affairs are sometimes called infatuations or in the case of young men "calf love." So universal is this phase at the end of adolescence that some communities encourage both men and women to give their desires full physical expression in temporary sexual associations. No doubt when you arrive at this stage of life, when the sleeping princess is ready to be waked by the kiss of the prince, you will read and discuss the whole subject and with it the proposals of Judge Lindsey and others on the subject of pre-marital sexual life and "companionate" or trial marriages. No reasoning person can lay down the law and say this is wrong, that is right, there must always be wide variety in men and in women, and their needs require a corresponding variation in the habits of life. Physical association, provided it is a genuine love relationship, cannot in itself be immoral if it brings no injury to others, though it may be amoral, that is belonging to no known moral code. In the course of history some civilizations have allowed promiscuity to men and not to women or to women and not to men, all have a definite moral code. Read at this time, if your other work will allow you, Robert Briffault's *The Mothers*. You will find in it a fund of knowledge of past and present moralities. The present age is very much one of experiment but it should be followed by one of understanding and ordered freedom. The economic difficulties which have postponed marriage for many men until the thirties and kept many women as wage-earners, denying them either marriage altogether or freedom from wage-earning to enjoy a home life, can now be settled. We need no longer have, for so many people, a cramped life in cities but can give all homes access to the country without loss of what are called the amenities of civilized life. This should lead to a renewal of the vital link between human life and other forms of more instinctive life. The one thing, however, which will contribute most to the shortening of this period of desire for promiscuity is the knowledge I have attempted to convey to you in these letters. Any young man or woman who has been reared in these difficult transition years from one era to another, should, if his mental capacity allows, put himself or herself through a period of careful self-analysis. Such enquiries into the past and the subsequent synthesis should cancel out many infatuations before they have gone very far. Laughter is an extraordinarily useful medicine if we apply it to ourselves, though often painful or even injurious if applied to us, except on rare occasions, by others. You will at this time, too, read and discuss the problem of prostitution or the use of the sexual organs for the purpose of monetary gain. The woman who sells her body in this way is of necessity purely objective to the act of coitus, the subjective life cannot be given any emotional or physical satisfaction. It cannot be denied that certain women are so psychologically constituted that the life attracts them but in well-organized communities, where early marriage is possible and extra-marital association is allowed under definite rules or taboos, or where polygamy is the normal way of life, prostitution as a profession is almost non-existent. In certain Greek states the temple virgins were employed in this way, the word virgin meaning a free or unmarried woman. From what is called a sociological point of view the story of the life of a London prostitute told by herself under the title of *To Beg I am Ashamed* is worthy of study by serious students of the subject.

In the time of enquiry and search after a way of life, you will also come across the question of homosexuality or the physical expression of love of man for man or woman for woman, which in the case of women is often called Lesbianism. So much light has been thrown upon the whole subject by the work of psycho-analysts, that it is quite reasonable to state that where there is homosexuality there is fixation of the personality at some spot in infancy or at any rate in the pre-pubertal years. With the one possible exception of those few human beings who have abnormal reproductive glands or sexual organs and are known as hermaphrodites. The ordinary run of homosexual can normalize himself or herself by clearing up his fixations, probably with greater ease if he secures temporary aid from an endocrinologist. The flow of libido from man to man or woman to woman is an enrichment to life and remains when the desire for physical association is discarded. It is well to remember that whatever may be the rule of life we allow ourselves, and incidentally our friends, after we are out of adolescence we have to consider the needs of men and women together. We cannot live to ourselves alone nor should one class benefit at the expense of another.

Nor can there be any doubt about the fact I have already tried to make clear to you, that we suffer personally and racially if we replace the friendship-love of adolescence by any form of partial sexual satisfaction. Even the habit of "necking" which is an over-emphasis of the pleasure in contact, derived from the association of an infant with its mother, may make more difficult the adjustment to a full partnership life at a later date.

Your affectionate friend

XIX

MY DEAR MARGARET,

In the map of life I have been attempting to sketch for you we have come to the point where marriage is the natural next step. For the woman whose body is physically mature and subjectively balanced, this means an association recognized by Church or State which leads almost at once to the establishment of a home and the arrival of children to form a family.

I promised to give you an example of religious ceremonial prior to entry into marriage. It is on record that the Babylonians and later the Greeks, at some period of their history, made it incumbent on all women to present themselves at the temple and there wait, sometimes for several months, until some worshipper chose to sleep with them for one night. During that night coitus took place and the woman could then terminate her stay at the temple, return to her home and accept an offer of marriage. There was of course no question of the man and woman being lovers or even friends. The act of union with a stranger expressed the idea that the reproductive function of the woman's body belonged to God. When she had symbolically offered herself to God for the future fulfilment of the function, she was free to enter into the human love relationship which has enriched so vastly what in animals is as you know a purely instinctive act. The woman's rhythm of life is normally one of eighteen months or longer. Conception followed by nine months during which the child is carried and another nine months or more during which it is fed from the breasts. A subjectively balanced woman (♀) can only neglect this rhythm at the peril of physical or spiritual disaster. An objective (♂) woman can adopt a man's rhythm, but if she does so to the neglect of her own, she is cutting herself off from further subjective development. If, on the other hand, she allows nature to take its course, subject to a necessary rest period between one child and the next, she may, after the arrival of the second or third child, develop the neglected subjective personality and gain a new understanding of life. An attempt was made a few years ago to get this truth across in the play *The Dominant Sex*: perhaps you will get the opportunity of seeing it at a repertory theatre or in one of those picture houses which specialize in classic films. For the same reason that there is in woman a memory of the male rhythm which enables her to find enjoyment in satisfying the physical needs of her mate, so in the man's mental life there is the memory of the woman's rhythm which influences his creative output both monthly and at nine-monthly intervals. The attraction which leads to marriage may be felt on the level of intellectual companionship or intuitional friendship or on that of emotional and physical attraction but in an ideal marriage the association becomes more and more complete, the man and woman alternating the objective and subjective relationship to each other according to their needs. There cannot by any possible means be similar growth in the man and woman, each must travel their own road, but with a tolerance and understanding which comes from the ever-renewed love association. Any form of competition for or jealousy of the male or female position makes love an impossibility. The act of coitus in human beings is not the instinctive act it is in animals, which takes place solely for the purpose of reproduction, but can be and should be a means of constant spiritual refreshment. The Roman Catholic Church includes marriage in their list of sacraments. Many people through ignorance make use of the act as a sort of dope, they are rather like the toper who always having a drink at his elbow is no judge of good wine. Sexual congress at its best brings into play every faculty of man and revives every physical and emotional memory from the first pleasure of the contact of our lips with our mothers' breasts to maturity. When this is understood the association is less frequent but also infinitely more satisfying in its results for the man and woman concerned and for providing a satisfying spiritual atmosphere in the home. In these days of conscious control of the procreative powers and a wider tolerance of pre-marital sexual experiments, there is less likelihood than in the past that a man and a woman should find themselves linked in marriage but impotent, that is, unable to function satisfactorily. When it does occur the Church and State both recognize a state of affairs which warrants the annulling of the marriage. In many cases of impotence, however, adequate and extended self-analysis leads to full normal functioning. With a widening practical experience of life and a deepening objective mental development the woman's road should continue evenly for some years. Then comes a time when if the subjective libido is not to show itself in an increase of bulk there is need for a rebirth. H. G. Wells has suggested universities for women of thirty-five and over. Such universities would provide opportunity for women to take up again the development of the subjective life in the creative arts and literature which had to be abandoned as they entered the objective male puberty—an opportunity, in fact, to do what the boy has to do between his tenth and thirteenth year, to surrender the urge to physical reproduction in the bearing of children and to substitute for it some form of mental creativity.

Just how this can be done without disrupting the family life is one of the problems which will have to be solved in the new age. Some races are, and as far as is known have always been, polygamous and much harm has been done to them in recent years in the attempt to impose upon them the European ideal of a monogamic life. Where formerly in these communities every woman had an opportunity to satisfy the subjective urge to reproduction they now substitute for it the totally inadequate satisfaction of an objective relationship often on a commercial basis. So natural is polygamy in parts of Africa that it is a frequent occurrence for a woman who finds that her children and her agricultural work are too much for her to go to her husband and say it is time for him to have a younger wife. The two women work very happily together and often after a few years encourage the husband to introduce a third wife into the home. Some way out of the difficulty must as I have already suggested be found, a way I mean which does not leave hundreds of women starved of companionship and the opportunity to live a full life. One that allows women to continue their individual development in their middle years of life but leaves the home as a central pivot. The solution will never be found in the break up of the home.

In the early years of this century there was a widespread idea that children were the property of the State and could be satisfactorily brought up in public crêches. There is no atom of evidence that such a thing is possible on a large scale. The home is the natural starting-point in life, a spiritual need for both men and women. The symbol of security from which children can go out exploring ever widening circles of life, with a confidence that they can return at any time until they finally break away to form a new family unit. The place where as children they can unconsciously learn from the continued functional life of the parents and give due homage to the lares and penates. For all these and many other environmental needs an institution is a very meagre substitute.

Your affectionate friend

XX

MY DEAR MARGARET,

I want now to tell you more about the road of life for the unanchored male. That is to say, the man who has had such an exceptionally satisfactory home and school life that he has been able to move from stage to stage without fixations, or one who has satisfactorily freed himself by an adequate self-analysis at the end of adolescence. It is necessary to think of men also as of two types as we did women, but we can only do so justifiably if at the same time we bear in mind that there is every variety of male, from the powerfully self-assertive to the man who is for the most part subjective and receptive. Some psychologists call the extremes the resistive and the sensitive types. I have pointed out to you that the road for women is a practical one—enrichment of the spiritual life by the subjective function of motherhood and the objective interests connected with the art of living. I purposely left out of the picture those half beings who in process of time are able to destroy all their subjective female life and become the efficient office worker or administrator—people not fully human, more efficient than a man but without the subjective side of the man's personality which allows him to remain human in his day-to-day relationship with those around him.

The physical life of a man is such that he can, if necessity arises, find a spiritual unity without experiencing the marriage relationship for even a short period of time, but the number of women who can do so is infinitely small. Many men who attempt to evade the normal experiences of life revert to some childish form of physical satisfaction, but a woman cannot function without the co-operation of a male and only a limited few of those who deliberately choose spinsterhood, even with the fullest help that religion can give them, are able to continue fully and progressively alive.

The task of both men and women after they have come of age, which in practice can be taken as nineteen for the woman and twenty-one for the man, is the same, to find a spiritual unity, but where the woman's road is, as I have explained to you, for the child-bearing phase of her life a practical one, that of the man is by unconscious subjective functioning. The great religions of the East, Hindoism, Buddhism, Taoism, and the mystical forms of Christianity, have been developed to help men to this end. I will return to the subject to tell you more about it in my next letter.

At about twenty-five years of age some men feel the urge to fatherhood: they discover that they want something more than companionship and the satisfaction of being "in love." To other men the desire comes much later and the arrival of children to the wives of these men is more an incident in their lives than a part of the process of self-fulfilment. To a subjective woman the knowledge that she is in child is a factor which gives her renewed confidence and there is a somewhat similar feeling on the part of the more sensitive men when they realize that their part in the act of procreation has become effectual. There is a recurrence of this feeling of pride at the birth of the child and this is increased for the father if the first child is a girl and for the mother if it is a boy. In very inverted personalities, that is, in those partnerships where the woman is very objective and the man subjective, this usual balance of interest is reversed, the woman sees herself completed in a daughter, the man in a son. The marriage relationship may for some people run smoothly for many years, but for some partners changes in the attitude of one necessitates willing readjustment on the part of the other. The absence of knowledge about these changes from the objective to the subjective attitude or *vice versa* has led in recent years to an enormous increase in the number of divorces. Their number in relation to the number of marriages should be very much less when psychological knowledge is general instead of confined to a very limited few. At the same time it is well to realize that if after what appears to be a happy start one partner continues to grow and the other becomes static or goes back to some infantile stage of life, substituting, for example, cruelty for love, there must be some way of escape and most countries or States have recognized this and provide for the legal dissolution of the marriage. Some people enter upon marriage intending the association to be no more than a partial and incomplete one. The film star who is giving all her libido in an outward objective way in her profession, moves from man to man in repeated divorces because though she is refusing the subjective life of child-bearing, she is at the same time unconsciously seeking a mate who will compel her to accept it. If, on the other hand, she marries a man who takes up her energy, her professional work suffers and she finds herself facing the problem of psychologically feeding him and giving up her profession, or breaking off the association in a separation or divorce.

When there is little or no change in the balance of personality during perhaps a quarter of a century of married life there may be a sudden turn round. The man, objective and positive for so many years, may pass through a phase similar to the climacteric of women and become receptive. The climacteric is that time in a woman's life when the ovaries cease to form egg cells. There are several Greek myths which have as their theme the loss of potency in the man, that is, the power of functioning in coitus and its ultimate renewal. For a normal male who has not used his reproductive glands to excess in the early years of life fatherhood is possible say from seventeen to seventy, and there is little doubt that the persistence of glandular activity gives the man a continued mental alertness which early impotence denies him. So intimate is the relationship between the physical and spiritual life that neither men nor women can afford to have inactive, that is to say, insensitive organs. Even if they are not put to full use in the intimacy of sexual companionship they should remain alive to day-to-day emotional reactions to friends and acquaintances.

Your affectionate friend

XXI

MY DEAR MARGARET,

I promised in this letter to return to the subject of the mental life of men after they have become adult. The idea of the duality of man or woman has long since ceased to be strange to you, but you must keep it always in mind otherwise men will be as much an enigma to you as your sex is generally held to be to men. In this truth lies the secret of all the higher religions, the search for unity, the synthesis of the subjective female personality with the objective male. I do not propose to write you a long dissertation on religions, nor am I qualified to do so. There is as I have shown you before a duality in them as in everything else. On the one hand, the objective symbolic approach through ritual and the male intuition and the subjective appreciation of truth through the development of an inner mystic life. Christianity has as you are aware both sides. Mohammedinism, which is also a development of the Hebrew teaching, has thrown off the subjective half and overemphasized the objective. In the age of chivalry the man's search for the subjective half of life was known as the search for the Holy Grail. If I give you a brief outline of the alchemistic teaching it will serve you as a guide, if later you wish to investigate teachings and practice of other religions. Alchemy was pre-Christian in origin but as it was presenting universal truth it was adopted as a vehicle of expression of Christianity and was widespread in Europe for over a thousand years. Those alchemists who made use of the objective approach to inner knowledge spent their time in primitive laboratories where they occupied themselves with heating up a variety of substances with the idea of turning them into gold. Those most frequently used were sulphur, salt and mercury; these were mixed with earth and occasionally other things were added. Now the chemical sign for mercury is the moon over the sun with a cross under it (☿) that stood for libido or spirit, neither male nor female or both whichever way you like to put it. Sulphur was male and salt female. Together they were the ever necessary three which was expressed by a triangle △. It is quite certain that at no time did an alchemist succeed in making gold from other substances, but the persistence of the effort and the constant re-enactment of the ritual developed the personality of the alchemist himself. The other kind of alchemist, the subjective, had no laboratory but used the chemical terms as a philosophical language. These men perceived and expressed the same truth that we now express in psychological terms but kept it hidden in the mystic garb of a symbolic language. The illustration which accompanies this letter is a photo-reproduction from a manuscript in the British Museum and is easily translated into psychological terms. Many similar illustrations are far more complicated and need extensive study before they can be adequately interpreted. The cube with the flowers round it is the physical instinctive life. Above that is shown by the symbols of the Sun, Moon, and Mercury the division of the personality into the male and female elements and the libido. These three are repeated in the next section in the form of a triangle. Within it is a phoenix rising from the flames. You will remember that the mythical phoenix is said to burn itself up every seven years and rise again from the ashes. This symbolizes the many rebirths through which both men and women go if they are living a full life. Finally, at the top we have Hermaphroditos the mystic or spiritual androgyne. Much of his reproductive energy is now given to his mental life, so the mercury symbol is shown over the sex organs, while the sun and moon, the male and female symbols, cover the breasts. In his hands Hermaphroditos, who is the gold of the objective alchemists, holds the symbols of time and measurement, while to the right and left of him appear the symbols of fire and water expressive of the objective ($♂$) and subjective ($♀$) difficulties which he has experienced in his life.

Hermaphroditos being formed from the interplay of

the three is sometimes given the number four. The triangle then becomes a □. It is probable that the same truth which is here expressed was part of the Jewish mystic teaching. The name for God which the English translations call Jehovah is said to be Yod-He-Vau-He, the four square, the Hermaphroditos of the alchemistic design. It is not everyone who is able to reach by the objective or subjective road the full development of the eight-sided personality but while we have life we struggle for fulfilment. The contribution to society of a great dramatic personality or a singer whose voice can take him round the world in Grand Opera has of necessity to give the greater part of his libido to one or two facets exclusively. This specialization occurs also in many individuals whose light has less brilliance. As a solution of the problem that this specialization presents the Buddhist philosophers developed a theory of reincarnation which holds the idea that the non-material element in man returns to earth again and again until everything has been experienced and the personality unified. I cannot deny or confirm the belief, I prefer to think that the experiences and trials we have missed may be made up for in some other place than Earth. On the other hand, it is well to remember that what the intuition has given out as truth at one time is often given reaffirmation in another and subsequent age, as a result of scientific and intellectual approach.

Man's journey from birth through numerous phases to full humanity has been told many times. You can read it in the story of Hercules, of Hiawatha, of Christian in Bunyan's *Pilgrim's Progress*, or in the oldest epic poem, the story of Gilgammesh, which has recently been translated into English. This story is possibly five thousand years old and has been found in the process of archaeological exploration of the temples of the Sumerians. The dual personality is described in it under the characters of Gilgammesh (♀) and Enkiou (♂). As mysticism belongs to the subjective female side of the personality this side of religion has been developed by men for men, but there are of course many who can learn only from the objective symbolic ritual approach. If in the coming age the subjective side of women can find a rebirth after a satisfying period of physical reproduction the world will be enriched by the addition of many to the ranks of creative artists and philosophers. By the word philosopher I do not mean the erudite professor of the subject but the average man or woman who functions subjectively on the intellectual level.

The woman's movement of the last half century has been action on the part of objective (♂) types of women to secure what they assumed was equality with man in the professional world. The work of the pioneers has done much to remove some of the disabilities of women in an age of materialism. Recently the more subjective type of woman has joined the professional ranks, but though she has a wider humanity, her conflict is greater and there are many who break down under the strain before middle age. What does it profit a woman if she gains the gold medal for surgery or a seat in Parliament if she loses her own soul?

The subjectively developed women must take a fuller share in ordering the new world so that due place is given to subjective functioning, and that necessitates a phase of life where there is for them a satisfying dependence and security.

Your affectionate friend

XXII

MY DEAR MARGARET,

With this letter I must return to tell you something more about the woman's road. I have often drawn your attention to the fact that the physical differentiation of males and females precludes the possibility of their travelling identical roads. Man's main contribution to the development of the human personality has been through the sublimation of his instinctive female desires, which has given him subjective mental creative activity (subjective imagination) expressed in all those forms which Plato included under the generic term "Poetry." The woman, on the other hand, must satisfy the subjective urges by the use of her body or they destroy her; the only alternative is suppression and an over-emphasized and one-sided personality. Woman then has to make her contribution on the objective male side and to her is due the objective imagination and the objective intellect both now part of the common heritage. When I was telling you about development in the early years of the male puberty, I mentioned the surrender on the part of girls of the desires connected with male reproductive activities. It is this inner gesture of surrender which enables women to develop the objective intuition and the objective intellect. Those who have not resolved that conflict are ever jealous of the male sexual activity and are often emotionally and physically violent, becoming the shrews and the sadists among women. But the woman who has made the surrender develops an objective power of giving which men have always considered her greatest glory. In myths and poetry men have ever eulogized this power. In Asia where water is a matter of life and death the favourite simile has been the life-giving spring or well at which men can find refreshment and rejuvenation. I recently came across a new translation of the works of Goethe, and this is how he expresses his appreciation of the quality:

> "What Woman's beauty to portray
> I deem it but a bootless task;
> Too oft it is alack-a-day
> An icy-chill and moreless marsh,
> But her alone can I account
> As lovely, be she maid or wife,
> From whom does flow, as from a fount,
> A stream of bright and gladsome life."

This outward flow of power is evident also in men and will be more so when the primitive forms of expression of power are discarded as barbaric. But there are many even among psychologists who cannot see power as anything higher than physical and emotional violence. Those men who have the power of

LETTERS TO MARGARET

spiritual healing have sublimated violence into this outward intuitional power of love. Jesus of Nazareth possessed it to a marked degree. If you read through St. Mark's Gospel you will note the many times he read the thoughts of those about him and healed many by the power of his love.

The importance of this difference of road for men and women has been overlooked, as many other matters of real importance to the human race and each individual have been overlooked in the age of materialism and rule by the immature.

The Persians at the time of their zenith dealt with the problem by giving women a completely separate life from men. There was no question of inferiority. Under the harem system the women had rights and privileges quite as definite as those of the man. Woman was not the property of man as she was for so long a period in Europe. It was left to the woman, for example, to say when she was desirous of physical association with her husband, and she intimated this by putting her shoes outside her door. From this custom came the phrase you must have come across sometimes, "Slipper rule." When the custom was adopted by the Arabs some time after the death of the prophet Mohammed, it was adopted as a cultural advance absorbed with other things as the Arabs became less crude in their habits. They did not, however, understand the significance of the separation and used the Purdah system as a method of forcing women into a receptive dependent position. At the present time the women of the East are throwing off the yoke and moving in the direction of "freedom" and "equality." There is, however, no advance in the swing of a pendulum and there is great danger that the women of Turkey, for instance, where the most rapid changes have taken place, will lose much that is of importance to them by attempting to travel the man's road. To neglect the subjective side of life will not only spell disaster for them, but will quite definitely not secure for them any real equality.

In England the educational system for boys is based on the monastic system and in recent years the girl's education has been intentionally copied from the boy's with results that are none the less disastrous because at present only vaguely appreciated. I have pointed out to you in an earlier letter that it is on the subjective side that women must make their next advance. In the age of conscious understanding, men and women should be able to plan an educational system adjusted to their special needs. The roads must of necessity be different from early adolescence but they can meet again for the mature in the latter half of life. It is not a question of denying women any position formerly held by men but of the time of life she can best occupy them, in her own interest and for the benefit of the race as a whole. The man's timetable has brought too many women to a breakdown before middle life. Even in the days of Persian leadership of culture, working women could not share in the independence allowed to the well-to-do class, but now that science has mastered production there should be opportunity of leisure for all. The world can and must abolish money slavery which in many ways has proved far more soul destroying than the chattel slavery it displaced. This terrible blight is spreading insidiously from Europe to the East. All seeing people hope that Asia will be able to absorb our scientific knowledge and apply it without the evils which have accompanied the expansion of industry in Europe.

The true "matron," the mother of adult or nearly adult children, can reach a stability of personality which in many civilizations has placed her on an equality with the wisest of men. If you look in the Book of Proverbs* in your *Bible intended to be read as Literature* you will find a summary of what were in the opinion of an ancient Hebrew writer the characteristics of a perfect woman; you will note that they are of an objective nature. This objectivity was balanced by a fully satisfied instinctual subjective life. An exclusively objective life even if expressed as love for a child or husband is poisonous, as all things are poisonous in excess, but to start to develop that theme for you would need many more letters. You

* See Appendix II.

can study it in later years, if you wish, in the psychological text-books.

In an age of conscious control, the instinctive subjective satisfaction must for women be augmented by the addition of mental subjectivity. An understanding world cannot allow the reduction of the over-plus of population by famine, flood or wars, by direct infanticide or infanticide through the neglect of adequate hygienic precautions. On the other hand, economic pressure must no longer deny any woman a satisfying physical life such as she obtained in an age of rule by the instincts.

Your affectionate friend

XXIII

MY DEAR MARGARET,

This is to be the last of the series of the letters that I promised to write for you. In them I have not set you any rules of life; that was not my province or my intention. Had I attempted to do so I would have stultified that very growth, physical and spiritual, which I hoped to release in you to find its own expression. Nor have I told you any new things. Truth is eternal, only the form of its expression changes. If in this letter I am to offer you any personal advice, it is to make use of all roads to knowledge available to you, nor would I have you except the primitive objective method of experiment, failure and re-trial. The four roads to understanding, the physical, emotional, intuitional, and intellectual, are known to you. Do not miss living by taking too much thought: it is better to make mistakes and acknowledge them than never to have dared to live. Many people of my generation and others who were born in the late nineteenth and early twentieth centuries have had no chart to guide them. Like Columbus we have had to sail uncharted seas, but no one would choose to do so. No one would risk his boat, passenger and crew in a voyage over a sea where the rocks and shoals were known without a chart if such a thing was available.

In my boyhood the religion of the Churches was so remote from the actualities of life that it was of very little help. Christianity had gone through a slow but steady process of divorce from political life and had long since abandoned any attempt to insist on the application of basic principles of right and justice. In fact, only a few outstanding personalities realized the dangerous road civilization was travelling. Details of ritual caused unholy dissensions between different branches of the Church and even different sections of the Church of England. Much time and ink was wasted over arguments about the verbal accuracy of the Hebrew and Christian literature which goes to form the Bible. The teaching of Jesus as to the power of the spirit and the psychological causes of many diseases had been discarded and for the most part the ministers and their congregations were materialists in practice, even when as individuals they had an intuitional appreciation of the meaning of unity and the God of Love. The God who was worshipped by the adherents to the other great religions of the world, and who had in his wisdom provided the less civilized races with a provisionally satisfying social environment in Africa and Polynesia and elsewhere, was considered to be a different being to the God of the white races. Missionaries were sent all over the world to disseminate European customs in the name of religion, often paving the way for those who could financially exploit the native races in the production of the raw materials of industry. The practice of national and international usury had successfully overcome the natural spiritual affinities of human beings. In the last quarter of a century a new understanding of God and his purpose has shown itself at many points. It is less than ten years ago that a synod of clergy of the Church of England dared to point out some of the immoralities inherent in the financial system. The next day, in a leading article, *The Times* told them in effect to run away and save souls and not concern themselves with other people's preserves. Now it is becoming very generally recognized that religion must have its social as well as its personal responsibilities. It remains to be seen to what extent the people of the new age can undo the evils perpetrated by those whose religion was more a habit and a dope than the embodiment of truth. When the symbolism of religion is not understood it loses much of its spiritual value and becomes a sort of magic. Psychological knowledge has given a new meaning to old customs and in so doing has reaffirmed their value, I am one of those who believe that the present period of disruption and disintegration will lead to a world-wide spiritual renaissance.

The rough chart which psychological work of

recent years has made it possible for me to give you, will not take from life the spirit of adventure. I could not, even if I wished to do so, protect you from the storms of wind and driving rain which are every mariner's lot, but I have attempted to indicate the position of the major snags.

It was at one time thought that conscience could be an adequate guide, but during the centuries of spiritual degradation the consciences of most people have become unreliable. But though conscience is not at the present moment of time a reliable guide, it is not necessary as some have suggested that the world should revert to an instinctive life. It is in my opinion important that there should be a period of conscious control, which will build up a new conscience. This will make life less of a strain for many generations yet to be born. In the first few years following the scientific discoveries of the last century about evolution in plants and animals, the newly found knowledge quite upset man's balance. It was so satisfying to feel that we were inevitably advancing towards an age of supermen, that no one seemed to stop to think if this was an accurate interpretation of the work of the Biologists. There is no reason to believe that the rules governing the evolution of the physical body apply in the mental or spiritual sphere. It is doubtful if man's physical body can change from the present pattern to any great extent, but in the psychological world he can regress as easily as progress. It is more than possible that knowledge can be found and used, lost and found again. There may have been civilizations of which there is no record much more enlightened in many directions than our own.

It has been suggested, for example, that there was at one time a continent in the Pacific of which all but the mountain tops are now beneath the sea and these are islands. Some of them have huge carved stones and other architectural remains, which were certainly not placed there or built by the present occupants of the islands or by anyone of their race who have preceded them.

Similar prehistoric remains are to be found in the valleys on the tops of the Andes in South America. Apparently the Sumerians who were in occupation of Babylonia five thousand years ago had originally come from a mountainous country and had built their temples on mountain tops. So innate was this custom that to satisfy their consciences they had to build artificial mountains called Ziggarats on which they then built their temples. It is not impossible that a race of men spread over a wide area of the earth's surface knew more than has since been known consciously about the human personality and that their disappearance owing to large scale disturbances of the earth's surface and perhaps decimation by more primitive invaders of their territory has necessitated a new climb up into an age of conscious understanding.

The recent scientific age has over-emphasized material and has neglected spiritual values. Insidiously the rule of money has asserted itself until all forms of government have had to acknowledge its overlordship. The pseudo-democracy of which we have boasted with more enthusiasm than judgment has not kept us from the inevitable breakdown. The rule of money has failed as it always must fail. That which gave apparent security has itself let loose a violence which is devastating Europe and may spread before the finish, until almost the whole population of the world is involved in conflict. Those who by their control of the monetary machine have held the destiny of civilization in their hands have proved themselves unfitted to control the vast power scientific research has made available for the production of material wealth.

Democracy as we have conceived it, not as we have applied it, is the most mature form of government. It gives to all the right of full development and expects from all functional service relative to their development. We should not despair of Democracy and turn to more primitive forms of government, but relegate both finance and big business each to their own province. A democratic people must see to it that the principles which guide their administrators are those which are appreciated by the higher level of the mind, and not those which have always governed the actions of money-lenders. Some of my generation may live to see the birth of the new age, but it is your generation which will have to impose the rules to govern its social and economic life; settle the principles on which can be provided an educational environment suitable to the needs of vital boys and girls; vitalize both family life and the communal religious life of the Churches so that there is no separate code for business and private use. As an aid to achieving these aims the conscious awareness of the psychological stages of individual human growth will be of the utmost importance.

A vista of constructive activity stretches out into the future. If you, the adolescents of to-day, can get free from your infantile attachments, you will refuse to rear the new civilization on the fear, greed and exploitation which have so long separated man from God.

When you first read some of these letters, you will only have partially understood them, and may even have been a little bored. Make it a habit of reading the whole series through on each of your birthdays until you are twenty-one years of age.

Your affectionate friend

APPENDIX I

Extract from *With Mystics and Magicians in Tibet*, by Alexandra David-Neel (London: John Lane The Bodley Head Ltd.), pp. 236—239.

"Yongden and I had spent the night in the open, sleeping in a ditch dug by the waters during successive rainy seasons, but for the moment dry and hardened by the frost. The lack of fuel had compelled us to start our daily tramp without drinking our usual hot buttered tea. So, hungry and thirsty, we walked till about noon when we saw, seated on his saddle carpet, near the road, a lama of respectable appearance who was finishing his daily meal. With him were three young *trapas* of distinguished mien, who looked more like disciples accompanying their master than common servants. Four fettered horses were trying to graze on some dry grass near the group.

The travellers had carried a bundle of wood with them and kindled a fire, a teapot was still steaming on the embers.

As befitted our assumed condition of beggarly pilgrims, we respectfully saluted the lama. Most likely, the desire that the sight of the teapot awakened in us could be read in our faces. The lama muttered *"ningje"* (How sad! Poor things! etc.) and, aloud, told us to sit down and bring out our bowls for tea and *tsampa*.

A *trapa* poured the remaining tea in our bowls, placed a bag of *tsampa* near us and went to help his companions who had begun to saddle the beasts and make ready to start. Then one of the horses suddenly took fright and ran away. This is a common occurrence, and a man went after the animal with a rope.

The lama was not talkative, he looked at the horse which

ran in the direction of a hamlet and said nothing. We continued to eat silently. Then, I noticed an empty wooden pot besmeared with curd and guessed that the lama had got the curd from a farm which I could see at some distance away from the road.

The diet of daily *tsampa* without any vegetables proved rather trying for the stomach and I availed myself of all opportunities to get milk food. I whispered in Yongden's ear: "When the lama is gone, you shall go to the farm and ask for a little curd."

Though I had spoken very low and we were not seated very near to the lama, he appeared to have heard my words. He cast a searching glance at me and again uttered *sotto voce* "ningjed"!

Then he turned his head in the direction where the horse had run away. The animal had not gone far, but was apparently in a playful mood and did not permit the *trapa* to capture it easily. At last it let him throw the rope round its neck and followed him quietly.

The lama remained motionless, gazing fixedly at the man who advanced toward us. Suddenly, the latter stopped, looked around and went to a boulder near by, where he tied his horse. Then he retraced his steps a little way and leaving the road, walked to the farm. After a while I saw him come back to his horse carrying something. When he reached us the "something" turned out to be a wooden pot full of curd. He did not give it to the lama, but held it in his hand, looking interrogatively at his master as if saying "Was that what you wanted? What am I to do with this curd?"

To this unspoken question the lama answered by an affirmative nod, and told the *trapa* to give me the curd.

The second incident which I will relate did not occur in

LETTERS TO MARGARET

Tibet itself, but on the borderland territory that has been annexed to the Chinese provinces of Szetchuan and Kansu.

At the skirt of the immense primeval forest that extends from Tagan to the Kunka pass, six travellers had joined my small party. The region is known as being haunted by daring Tibetan robbers, and those who must cross it look for opportunities of forming as large and as well-armed a company as possible. Five of my new companions were Chinese traders, the sixth was a Bonpo *ngagspa*, a tall man whose long hair, wrapped in a piece of red material, formed a voluminous turban.

Anxious to glean anything that I could regarding the religion of the country, I invited the man to share our meals in order to find an opportunity of chatting with him. I learned that he was going to join his master, a Bonpo magician who was performing a great *dubthab* on a neighbouring hill. The object of this rite was to coerce a malignant demon who habitually harmed one of the small tribes which live in that region. After diplomatic preambles I expressed my desire of paying a visit to the magician, but his disciple declared the thing utterly impossible. His master must not be disturbed during the full lunar month necessary to perform the rite.

I understood that it was useless to argue with him, but I planned to follow him when he parted with us, after crossing the pass. If I succeeded in coming unexpectedly upon the magician, I might perhaps have a glimpse at him and at his magic circle. Consequently I ordered my servants to keep good watch on the *ngagspa* so that he could not leave us unnoticed.

Probably they spoke too loudly among themselves about the matter. The *ngagspa* saw through the trick I intended playing upon his *guru* and told me it was no use attempting it.

I replied that I did not harbour any evil intention against

his master and only wanted to have a talk with him for the sake of enlightenment. I also commanded my servants to keep a still closer watch on our companion. The *ngagspa* could not be aware that he had become a prisoner. But as he also understood that no harm would be done to him and that he was well fed—a thing to which Tibetans are keenly alive—he took his adventure good humouredly.

"Do not fear that I shall run away," he said to me. "You may bind me with ropes if it pleases you. I need not go ahead to inform my master of your coming. He already knows all about it. *Ngais lung gi teng la len tang tsar.*" (I have sent a message on the wind.)

Ngagspas are in the habit of boasting of so many and such various miraculous powers that I did not pay any more attention to his words than to those of his colleagues in the black art.

This time I was wrong.

When we had crossed the pass, we entered a region of pasture land. Robbers were not much to be feared on these wide table lands. The Chinese traders, who had clung to us day and night while in the forest, recovered their assurance and took leave. I still intended to follow the *ngagspa*, when a troup numbering half a dozen riders emerged from an undulation of the ground. They rode at full speed towards me, and dismounted, saluted, offered "*kha-tags*" (complimentary scarves) and a present of butter. After the polite demonstrations were ended, an elderly man told me that the great Bonpo *ngagspa* had sent them and begged me to renounce my intention of visiting him, for no one but an initiated disciple ought to approach the place where he had built his secret magic *kyilkhor*.

I had to give up my plan. The *ngagspa*, it seemed, had really informed his master by "sending a message on the wind." To persist would have been useless.

APPENDIX II

A HEBREW CONCEPTION OF AN IDEAL WOMAN

A virtuous woman who can find?
For her price is far above rubies.
The heart of her husband trusteth in her.
And he shall have no lack of gain.
She doeth him good and not evil
All the days of her life.
She seeketh wool and flax,
And worketh willingly with her hands.
She is like the merchant ships;
She bringeth her food from afar.
She riseth also while it is yet night,
And giveth meat to her household,
And their tasks to her maidens.
She considereth a field and buyeth it:
With the fruit of her hands she planteth a vineyard.
She girdeth her loins with strength,
And maketh strong her arms.
She perceiveth that her merchandise is profitable,
Her lamp goeth not out by night.
She layeth her hands to the distaff,
And her hands hold the spindle.
She spreadeth out her hands to the poor;
Yea, she reacheth forth her hands to the needy,
She is not afraid of the snow for her household;
For all her household are clothed with scarlet.
She maketh for herself carpets of tapestry

Her clothing is fine linen and purple.
Her husband is known in the gates,
When he sitteth among the elders of the land.
She maketh linen garments and selleth them;
And delivereth girdles unto the merchant.
Strength and dignity are her clothing;
And she laughs at the time to come.
She openeth her mouth with wisdom;
And the law of kindness is on her tongue.
She looketh well to the ways of her household,
And eateth not the bread of idleness.
Her children rise up and call her blessed;
Her husband also and he praiseth her, saying;
"Many daughters have done virtuously,
But thou excellest them all."
Favour is deceitful and beauty is ruin:
But a woman that feareth the Lord, she shall be praised.
Give her the fruit of her hands;
And let her works praise her in the gates.

      Anon. From the Book of Proverbs.